DRIVING PLATO'S CHARIOT

DRIVING PLATO'S CHARIOT

Lessons on Student Ethical Development

GARY PAVELA, DeFOREST McDUFF,
GREGORY PAVELA, AND JUSTIN COEN

eBook ISBN: 979-8-9909274-0-7
Paperback ISBN: 979-8-9909274-1-4

Gary Pavela

Gary Pavela, JD, is a co-founder of the Academic Integrity Seminar. He received his law degree from the University of Illinois and was a Fellow at the University of Wisconsin Center for Behavioral Science and Law. He clerked for Judge Alfred Murrah of the U.S. Court of Appeals for the Tenth Circuit and taught at the Federal Judicial Center in Washington, D.C. (the training arm of the United States Courts). Gary was designated a Fellow of the National Association of College and University Attorneys (individuals who have "brought distinction to higher education and to the practice of law on behalf of colleges and universities across the nation"), and he served on the Board of the Kenan Institute for Ethics at Duke University.

DeForest McDuff

DeForest McDuff, PhD, is a co-founder of the Academic Integrity Seminar. His doctorate in economics is from Princeton University, where he was a winner of the Towbes Teaching Prize for outstanding undergraduate teaching. He works as an economic consultant at Insight Economics (an economic consulting firm he founded in 2017), and he is an Assistant Teaching Professor in the Department of Economics at the University of North Carolina at Chapel Hill.

Gregory Pavela

Gregory Pavela has a PhD in sociology from the University of Florida. He serves as Associate Dean for Academic Affairs in the School of Public Health at the University of Alabama at Birmingham (UAB) and is a past Chair of the Ethics Section, American Public Health Association. Greg received the President's Award for Excellence in Teaching at UAB as well as the Graduate Dean's Excellence in Mentorship Award.

Justin Coen

Justin Coen has a JD from Duke University and undergraduate degrees in accounting and English from the University of Maryland. While at Maryland, Justin served as the Chair of the Student Honor Council and was instrumental in developing the university's Honor Pledge. He has advised the U.S. Senate Committee on Finance and later served as a senior regulatory attorney at the Office of the Staff Judge Advocate (JAG), U.S. Army Medical Research and Development Command. He is currently a partner in the Washington, D.C. office of the Venable Law firm.

To my three sons: *Gregory*, *Hunter*, and *James* and a rising new generation: *Julia*, *William*, and *Conrad*. May all your lives be filled with as much joy and beauty as you have given to me.
-- Gary Pavela

To Gary, for being an incredible teacher, mentor, and friend; for teaching me about the importance of truth, honesty, and integrity; and for helping me to reflect on life's big questions.
-- DeForest McDuff

To my wife: Hyeyoung, and my parents, brothers, and students--who bring meaning to my work.
-- Greg Pavela

For Ashley, Willa, and Beatrix.
--Justin Coen

All four authors also wish to acknowledge the magnificent support received from our fellow Academic Integrity Seminar tutors and colleagues, Anastasia Pavela and Lee Elkins. Thousands of Seminar students have benefited from their guidance. This book and our Seminar would not have been possible without them.

Nature has two voices, the one is high, the other low; one is in sweet accord with reason and justice, and the other apparently at war with both.
--Frederick Douglass

One can dispose of one's drives like a gardener and, though few know it, cultivate the shoots of anger, pity, [and] vanity, as productively and profitably as a beautiful fruit tree on a trellis.
--Friedrich Nietzsche

CONTENTS

Public Domain

Of the nature of the soul let me speak briefly, and in a figure. And let the figure be composite—a pair of winged horses and a charioteer. Now the winged horses and the charioteers of the gods are all of them noble ... but the human charioteer drives his in a pair; and one of them is noble and the other is ignoble; and the driving of them of necessity gives a great deal of trouble to him.[1]

From Plato's *Phaedrus*
(the vase image interpreted)

---

1   Plato, Phaedrus (Jowett, trans., 2012) p. 14.

INTRODUCTION

How would you design a required course on academic integrity for thousands of college students who did not want to take it? If the course turned out to be measurably successful, what insights could be shared with other educators?

The four authors of this book --accomplished professionals in applied ethics, public health, economics, and law-- focus on those two questions. What we have learned goes beyond issues related to academic integrity and encompasses a broad range of ethical development programming at schools and colleges.

Over 45,000 students have completed the Academic Integrity Seminar (AIS) and related programs.[2] Referring schools include a mix of leading public and private institutions nationwide.[3] Student success in AIS has been demonstrated by survey results included in the "AIS Performance Report" (online appendix) and by hundreds of pages of student comments [4] like this one:

---

2   Our related programs include a series of Seminars titled "Vanderbilt Trust" at Vanderbilt University (affirming and teaching the value of trust) and the "Pocket Guide to Academic Integrity" (an instructional module designed to introduce the basic principles of academic integrity, completed by over 10,500 students so far).

3   Referring institutions have included Purdue, Stanford, Vanderbilt, Tufts, MIT, Ohio State, The University of North Georgia, Lehigh, the University of Iowa, Loyola University, Rutgers, Georgia Institute of Technology, George Mason University, Miami University, the University of Texas, Embry–Riddle Aeronautical University, the University of South Carolina, Babson College, the College of Charleston, Oberlin College, Virginia Tech, Appalachian State University, University of Mary Washington, the University of Rochester, The University of North Carolina Wilmington, UC-Davis, and UC-Berkeley.

4   Comments volunteered by AIS students can be viewed at this source on the AIS website.

> *I just want to say, wow, this seminar was nothing like I expected. At first, I thought this seminar would be like punishment and busy work, but as soon as I started it, I realized that it was much more. The assignments were thought provoking and inspirational and I could feel myself wanting to try and become someone people can look up to . . . . This whole little journey actually really opened my eyes more about who I want to be, how I want to approach it, and how I want to thank the people in my life. Thank you so much for the comments and everything!*

What this student learned--and how that learning was designed and communicated--is the focus of our book.

AIS provides basic instruction on how academic dishonesty is defined, but our primary goal has been helping students understand why academic integrity is *important.* The latter task necessarily entails deep engagement with applied ethics and purposeful learning, including topics identified in our chapter titles: *Gratitude; Know Thyself (Self-insight and Self-management); Trust; Truth-telling and Professional Responsibility;* and *Joyfulness, Purpose, and Fulfillment.* Our opening chapter on *The Power of Stories* explains the pedagogy pertaining to each of these topics.

Self-discovery and the chariot metaphor

Applied ethics and purposeful learning can't be taught by precept. A journey in self-discovery is required. The best that can be achieved in any such effort was described by microbiologist René Dubos (who is also featured in Chapter One):

> Every perceptive adult knows he is part beast and part saint, a mixture of folly and reason, love and hate, courage and cowardice. He can be at the same time believer and doubter, idealist and skeptic, altruistic citizen and selfish hedonist. The coexistence of these conflicting traits naturally causes tension but it is nonetheless compatible with sanity. In a mysterious way, the search for identity and the pursuit of self-selected goals harmonize opposites and facilitate the integration of discordant human traits into some kind of working accord. [5]

---

5   Dubos, René, *A God Within* (1972), p. 84.

Dubos's description of the need to manage "conflicting traits" in the human psyche explains why Plato's chariot allegory is an important theme throughout this book. The allegory depicts a charioteer (representing higher levels of reason and understanding) who must control two horses--one with an orientation toward moral goodness and the other driven by selfish desires.

Defining an admirable life

AIS students aren't encouraged to pursue the fruitless endeavor of finding and maintaining a perfect balance in life. Instead, we introduce them to thought experiments, psychological insights, philosophical perspectives, and "lives of integrity"--including Charles Darwin, Abraham Lincoln, Frederick Douglass, and Nelson Mandela--so they might identify better ways to create a "working accord" that brings them closer to an *admirable life*. An admirable life, we suggest, is distinguished by the responsibility it assumes; the courage and resilience it exemplifies; the compassion it displays; the wisdom it develops; the trust it inspires; and the beauty it creates.[6]

I believe this Academic Integrity Seminar should be incorporated into every university's pre-freshman coursework the summer prior. The lessons learned from the various readings are immense. It allows the individual to self-reflect on the choices they have made in the past and what choices they will make in the future. I would hope everyone who has the opportunity to take the Seminar keeps an open mind because they will garner so much wisdom which can be incorporated into their lives for years to come.

--AIS student comment

---

6   This language is drawn, in part, from Gary Pavela's MEDIUM essay "An Introduction to Aristotle's Ethics" (February 2023).

Many AIS readings and assignments are drawn from the humanities. We also introduce students to thinkers in interdisciplinary fields who build conceptual bridges between disciplines, including Martha Nussbaum, Richard Feynman, Carol S. Dweck, Charles Darwin, Robert Sapolsky, Antonio Damasio, Jonathan Haidt, Mark Edmundson, and E. O. Wilson.

Students will discover, for example, that Charles Darwin was a pre-eminent biologist, a leading thinker on applied ethics, and an advocate of the methodology of science--all while struggling with lifelong challenges to his physical and mental health (see our MEDIUM article in the online Appendix: Charles Darwin: A Study in Resilience, Adaptation, and Purpose).

Exploring foundational topics in multiple fields

Declining enrollments in the humanities should motivate educators in every discipline to devote more time to exploring foundational topics in their fields. What do they find fascinating, inspiring, and beautiful about what they teach?

Here are several examples of foundational topics in science, engineering, and business included in the Academic Integrity Seminar:

- **Johannes Kepler** asked the question *"Why are things as they are and not otherwise?"* [7]

    What does Kepler's inquiry suggest about the importance of using imagination and reason to explore any subject in depth?

- **E. O. Wilson** (Pellegrino University Research Professor Emeritus at Harvard University and winner of the National Medal of Science) wrote that *"the most successful scientist thinks like a poet—wide-ranging, sometimes fantastical—and works like a bookkeeper."* [8]

    How can students cultivate and balance those two qualities in themselves?

---

7   Kepler, Johannes, cited in "Leibnitz, World of Math."

8   Wilson, E. O., *The Meaning of Human Existence* (2014), p. 41.

- **Albert Einstein, Richard Feynman, and Charles Darwin** wrote evocatively about insights drawn from the sciences:

  Einstein: "*The most beautiful experience we can have is the mysterious. It is the fundamental emotion that stands at the cradle of true art and true science.*" [9]

  Feynman: "*Imagination reaches out repeatedly trying to achieve some higher level of understanding, until suddenly I find myself momentarily alone before one new corner of nature's pattern of beauty and true majesty revealed.*" [10]

  Darwin: "*Thus, from the war of nature, from famine and death, the most exalted object which we are capable of conceiving, namely, the production of the higher animals, directly follows . . . . [W]hilst this planet has gone cycling on according to the fixed law of gravity, from so simple a beginning endless forms most beautiful and most wonderful have been, and are being, evolved.*" [11]

  Some of the greatest scientists in history have used words like "imagination," "beautiful," "mysterious," and "wonderful" to describe their work. Do teaching and learning on college campuses encompass that vocabulary? If not, why not?

- **The Wright brothers** are two of the greatest engineers in American history. They developed a style of self-correcting argumentation summarized by Wilbur Wright:

  No truth is without some mixture of error, and no error so false that it possesses no element of truth . . . . Honest argument is

---

9   Einstein, Albert, "The World As I See It" (first published in 1934). Einstein also observed in the same essay:

> A knowledge of the existence of something we cannot penetrate, our perceptions of the profoundest reason and the most radiant beauty, which only in their most primitive forms are accessible to our minds: it is this knowledge and this emotion that constitute true religiosity. In this sense, and only this sense, I am a deeply religious man . . . . I am satisfied with the mystery of life's eternity and with a knowledge, a sense, of the marvelous structure of existence--as well as the humble attempt to understand even a tiny portion of the Reason that manifests itself in nature.

10   Feynman, Richard, Nobel Banquet Speech (1965).

11   Darwin, Charles, *Origin of Species*: second British edition (1860), p. 490.

merely a process of mutually picking the beams and motes out of each other's eyes so both can see clearly.[12]

What does Wright's observation reveal about the importance of truth-seeking and truth-telling in any discipline?

- **Ralph Gomory** (a research professor at New York University's Stern School of Business and winner of the National Medal of Science) wrote that:

  Evolution has produced two sides of human nature: the more self-centered and the more altruistic. Different training and circumstances can bring out in us more of one or the other, but they are both in our DNA.[13]

  How often and at what depth is human nature explored in schools of business or other academic fields nationwide?

Students who are fixated on career preparation are unlikely to ponder such questions. Consequently, they may miss out on experiencing the intrinsic joy of learning for its own sake--one of the most effective deterrents to academic dishonesty.

Our Seminar is too brief an exercise to provide a comprehensive alternative, but we can be an impetus for change. So, to create a more enduring impact, we urge students to pursue campus-based options, including identifying faculty mentors and asking them questions like *"What aspects of your field do you find most interesting?"* and *"What mysteries do you explore?"*

Learning from the Stanford "What Matters to Me and Why" forums

Our efforts to form a partnership with colleagues at referring institutions works both ways. Stanford students, for example, may be surprised to discover that some of the topics we examine with them were inspired by the "What Matters to Me and Why" forums on their

---

12   Tobin, James, *To Conquer the Air* (2004), p. 90.

13   Gomoroy, Ralph, "Put human nature back in business," *Washington Post* (June 28, 2013).

campus.[14] In that context, our role is to help reiterate insights and interventions other educators have taught us.

Old bureaucrat, my comrade, it is not you who are to blame. No one ever helped you to escape .... You have chosen not to be perturbed by great problems, having trouble enough to forget your own fate as man. You are not a dweller upon an errant planet and do not ask yourself questions to which there are no answers .... Nobody grasped you by the shoulder while there was still time. Now the clay of which you were shaped has dried and hardened, and naught in you will ever awaken the sleeping musician, the poet, the astronomer that possibly inhabited you in the beginning.[15]

-- Antoine de Saint-Exupéry

We've been surprised how many students tell us they are rarely asked to read, analyze, and express an informed opinion about historical, philosophical, or imaginative literature. How can we expect them to define a sense of meaning and purpose [16] without that opportunity? Many may be well prepared to begin their careers, but few will have thought deeply about what makes a career meaningful.

14　See the Stanford University link: "What Matters to Me and Why". See also a comparable program at the University of California, Irvine.

15　De Saint Exupery, Antoine, *Airman's Odyssey* (2012), p.12.

16　The critical role of a sense of meaning was expressed by Arthur C. Brooks in the September 12, 2023 *Atlantic* article "Three Myths and Four Truths About How to Get Happier:"

　　We can make do without enjoyment for a while, and even with little satisfaction. But if we lack meaning—which takes a lot of effort and sacrifice to find—we are utterly lost. Without it, we can't navigate life's inevitable challenges and crises. When we do have a sense of meaning, we can face life with hope and inner peace.

AIS SAMPLE EXERCISE

AIS tutors frequently invite students to undertake an unusual thought experiment:

Please take a tour through a local graveyard and see how many gravestone epitaphs you can find like this:

> *John will be long remembered and admired for developing a clever financial product that duped thousands of old people out of their life savings.*

Why don't we find more candid gravestones like John's? His financial product may not have been illegal--at least initially. And he can't go to jail because he's dead. If human connection and trust are irrelevant (i.e., only money and power are perceived to count), why should people like John hesitate to proclaim their financial "cleverness" for all to see?

Bottom line: human beings are highly cooperative social animals. We want to be remembered for the lives we've improved, the trust we've built, and the beauty we've created (our social instincts), not what we consumed or destroyed (our selfish instincts).

Encouraging student writing and thoughtful introspection

AIS assignments necessarily go beyond reading to encompass writing. We understand the temptations associated with generative AI and seek to develop assignments students find inherently engaging and worthwhile.[17] Most students understand, for example, that generative AI can write an embarrassingly clichéd "gratitude statement," [18] but that it can't feel or convincingly express individualized experiences that inspire love and admiration for particular individuals. AI deficiencies in this regard (among others) are demonstrated to students when we ask them to include *and analyze* pertinent ChatGPT responses in selected AIS assignments.

AIS students are also urged to consider the immediate personal benefit of doing their own thinking and writing.[19] Here's a pertinent observation from an AIS tutor to a UT-Austin student:

---

17   See, generally, McMurtrie, Beth, "What Will Determine AI's Impact on College Teaching? 5 Signs to Watch" *Chronicle of Higher Education*, September 8, 2023. McMurtrie cited two thoughtful observers on the topic:

> Gary Marcus, an emeritus professor of psychology and neuroscience at New York University . . . has become a leading [critical] voice on AI . . . Marcus wrote on Substack [that] ChatGPT went from being mistaken for a form of artificial intelligence that could learn and think "to being the butt of a joke, and an insulting shorthand for robotic, incoherent, unreliable, and untrustworthy . . . ."

***

> In higher ed, say educational developers, courses largely focused around rote skills and content memorization could become redundant. Think of large introductory classes, for example, with multiple-choice exams testing the ability to remember formulas and facts. Or poorly designed writing courses in which generic prose is considered passable . . . .
>
> *Courses that are not interdisciplinary, that don't focus on digging into evidence, that shy away from asking students what they value,* and that instead are "just kind of hand-waving and say, 'Well, evidence says X, Y, Z,' could become far less useful," says [Michael] McCreary [an educational developer at Goucher College who has written about the evolution and future of AI]. "We may need to find a way in higher ed of helping students to get some of that content so they can move on to other skills."

See also note 18.

18   Here's the ChatGPT response to our September 9, 2023 inquiry: *Please write a gratitude statement using the words of a typical college student*

> "Yo, I just wanna give a huge shoutout to all the people who've had my back during this wild college journey. From my professors who've dropped knowledge bombs and challenged me to grow, to my amazing friends who've been there for the late-night study sessions and spontaneous adventures, and to my family who've supported me through the ups and downs. I can't even express how grateful I am for this ride, the memories, and the growth. College wouldn't have been the same without you all. Much love and thanks!" 🎓🙏❤️ [emoji helpfully provided by Chat].

19   See Zimmerman, Jonathan, Here's my AI policy for students: I don't have one, *Washington Post*, August 29, 2023:

AIS TUTOR COMMENT

Our reflective writing exercises might be a model for what you can do on your own. Try writing in a personal journal every day for a week or so and see how it makes you feel. Do you gain added insight into yourself and others? Do you see previously missed connections between different ideas or events? Does your mind feel more focused and in flow? We've been influenced by the related work of James Pennebaker, Professor Emeritus of Psychology at the University of Texas. Please see his UT web page: *Click the link "Writing and Health." Here's a* related example *about how President Obama used daily reflective writing when he was a young man.*[20]

Most AIS writing exercises require thoughtful introspection. In one assignment, students are asked to follow the style of Stoic philosopher and Roman Emperor Marcus Aurelius when he wrote private thoughts of admiration about friends, teachers, and family members. We remind them that Marcus's effort was a "written meditation" designed to remember role models in the past and to habituate thoughts about worthy people and beautiful characteristics in the present. The latter perspective reflects Marcus's view (consistent with aspects of contemporary Cognitive Behavioral Therapy) that "the things you think about determine the quality of your mind. Your soul takes on the color of your thoughts." [21]

I will readily (and unhappily) admit that many college classes don't help you figure out what you really believe in. They reward students who spit back what the book or the professor says. You might as well be a robot. So I don't blame you if you draw on an actual robot to do the work for you.

But some courses really do ask you to think. And if you ask an AI bot to do it instead, you are cheating yourself. You are missing out on the chance to decide what kind of life is worth living and how you are going to live it.

20   See Pennebaker, James, "Writing and Health: Some Practical Advice" (viewed August 2023) and "Obama's Secret to Surviving the White House Years: Books," *New York Times*, January 16, 2017.

21   Aurelius, Marcus, *Meditations* (Hays, trans.; 2002), Book 5.16, p. 59.

> *The most valuable reading for me was Book I of*
> *Meditations by Marcus Arelius. I liked this excerpt so much*
> *that I read the next five books. The first book, especially,*
> *gave me a perspective of the traits that we typically*
> *value most in family and friends. Marcus doesn't express*
> *gratitude for people being interesting to him, but for*
> *having strong principles and good natures. This reading*
> *made me realize that the people in our lives who show*
> *inner peace and kindness towards others are the ones*
> *with the greatest impact on us.*
>
> --AIS student comment

One of our co-authors has written a book about college student suicide featured in the *Chronicle of Higher Education.*[22] Referenced in that book is a case study in which a student left notes revealing patterns of thinking before he died (anonymous disclosure of excerpts was authorized by the student's family for suicide prevention education).[23] It's painful to read instances when the student tapped into the executive function of his mind and--like a car ignition struggling but failing to start--*almost* achieved better self-insight. He wrote, for example, *"Will I ever cure stuttering? Job interviews, phone calls. People notice or am I blowing this out of proportion?"* Family and friends subsequently reported he was indeed "blowing this out of proportion."

Mark Edmundson (author of *The Age of Guilt: The Super-Ego in the Online World*) wrote in this regard:

Freud believed that when we turn mute inner experience into words, we begin to make progress. There's something about

---

22   Hoover, Eric, "Giving Them the Help They Need," *Chronicle of Higher Education*, May 19, 2006.

23   Publication of excerpts from the notes (without naming the student who wrote them) was supported by the student's parents in the hope that doing so might contribute to greater understanding of youth suicide and strategies to prevent it. Confirming correspondence dated December 22, 2011 was sent from the student's mother to Gary Pavela (on file).

expression that liberates. We can calm down and move with circumspection.[24]

Teachers are not substitutes for professional therapists. We can, however, help troubled students become sufficiently self-aware so they're motivated to seek help when they need it. This prospect is reiterated in the following observation shared with students by AIS tutors: *"Charles Darwin and Abraham Lincoln sought help for what they recognized could be debilitating mood disorders; that help--more readily available now from mental health professionals--enabled them to find a sense of purpose that defined them and enriched the world."*

When an educator asks a young person to think about developing a direction, it may cause confusion, even anxiety. But it is extremely healthy for the young person to be faced with these kinds of issues .... One of the endless sources of pain for me when I talk with young people who are struggling with their lives is the central theme of meaninglessness ... they are absent in terms of values, thinking, and direction. [25]

-- Samuel C. Klagsbrun, MD, Professor, Department of Psychiatry at the Albert Einstein College of Medicine (from an interview with Gary Pavela).

Lessons from the Harvard "Grant Study" on human flourishing

AIS tutors make frequent reference to lessons learned in the Harvard University "Grant Study" of adult development--also discussed in Chapter Six (Joyfulness, Purpose, and Fulfillment). An overview by

---

24   Edmundson, Mark, "Students, Meet the Superego," Inside higher Education (May 10, 2023).

25   Klagsbrun, Samuel, interview by Gary Pavela in *Synthesis: Law & Policy in Higher Education* (Summer 2002), p. 983.

long-time study director George E. Vaillant, M.D. was summarized in a 2001 *Harvard Magazine* article:

> [A]lthough it is not easy to change our defenses by ourselves, chance favors a prepared mind: "We can start by admiring how other skillful people cope. Then ponder, when things go badly for us, how we might have used self-defeating mechanisms." Lastly, [Vaillant] says, "consider this rule of thumb: *Don't try to think less of yourself, but try to think of yourself less*" [emphasis added].[26]

Overall, we're likely to *think of ourselves less* when we're expressing gratitude, deeply engaged in learning and exploring, experiencing awe and beauty, emulating "lives of integrity," expanding our capacity for trust, and devoting ourselves to a compassionate cause greater than ourselves.

[H]umor helps, and a sense of proportion. I am one individual on a small planet in a little solar system in one of the galaxies.[27]

--Roberto Assagioli

A concluding example

We end this introduction the way we end many of our tutor comments--with Albert Camus's example of human flourishing in his novel *The Plague*. A character in the novel, Dr. Rieux, had been fighting a relentless plague and reflected about the experience:

> Dr. Rieux resolved to compile this chronicle, so that he should not be one of those who hold their peace but should bear witness in favor of those plague-stricken people; so that some memorial of the injustice and outrage done to them might

---

26   Lambert, Craig, "The Talent for Aging Well," *Harvard Magazine* (March-April 2001). See also Wolf Shenk, Joshua, "What Makes Us Happy," *Atlantic* (June 2009).

27   Assagioli, Roberto, interview by Sam Keen in "The Golden Mean of Roberto Assagioli," *Psychology Today* (December 1974).

endure; and to state quite simply what we learn in time of pestilence: that there are more things to admire in men than to despise . . . . Nonetheless, he knew that the tale he had to tell could not be one of final victory. It could only be the record of what had had to be done, and what assuredly would have to be done again in the never ending fight against terror and its relentless onslaughts, despite their personal afflictions, by all who, *while unable to be saints, but refusing to bow down to pestilences, strive their utmost to be healers* [emphasis added].[28]

In many years of designing and teaching AIS assignments, we've found no better insight to share with our students.

---

28   Camus, Albert, *The Plague* (1991), p.308.

CHAPTER ONE

THE POWER OF STORIES

God made man because He loves stories.
Elie Wiesel

Human beings as storytelling animals

Greek gods like those named in the Apollo moon landings and NASA's more recent Artemis space mission have been part of the human imagination for thousands of years. Why do we continue to use them to personify some of our most important aspirations?

The answer highlights a quality of human nature: *our minds require stories to help us define goals, empower imagination, shape character, inspire empathy, and form cohesive bonds with others.* Human beings, in short, are preeminently storytelling animals.[1] The Academic Integrity Seminar is grounded on that premise. Most of our assignments immerse students in a story. We'll explore several of those stories here and in subsequent chapters.

Stories students tell about themselves

Our seminar is filled with stories, including stories about the truth-telling integrity of Frederick Douglass and a Confucian metaphor about goodness in human nature. Two of our stories, however, invite students to tell stories *about themselves:* how they wish to be perceived in the future (the Retirement Banquet exercise*)* and people to whom they are most grateful (The Gratitude Statement). Instead of a didactic lecture from a teacher, these assignments invite students to discover and empower the better angels of their own nature.

---

1   We draw upon multiple sources for this perspective, including Jonathan Gottschall, The Storytelling Animal: How Stories Make Us Human (2013) and Will Storr, The Science of Storytelling: Why Stories Make Us Human and How to Tell Them Better (2020).

TWO SAMPLE AIS EXERCISES

The Retirement Banquet

Please pretend you're at a retirement banquet. This is a serious and formal occasion, not a "roast." The person retiring is 70 years old and at the end of a long career. You know this person well--both inside and outside the workplace. It's your job to say a few truthful descriptive words about them. *What character or personality traits come to mind?*

> **Question for you to answer:** Pretend the person retiring is you. In short, we're asking you to project yourself into the future and to identify *at least five* descriptive words you hope others would say about you at a comparable event.

Comment: *No student so far--out of many thousands completing the seminar--has shared an aspiration to be known as a skillful liar or a master of economic exploitation. Instead, most write a story similar to this example from "Jane" (a pseudonym):*

> *Jane is one of the most caring souls I have ever met. She is a leader and has spent her whole life helping and leading others into a bright future. She is tenacious with everything she does and has a fire in her, a powerful sense of determination in her for accomplishing any of her goals. Unlike many people in today's world, she is also optimistic, a light to many others. Whether it's a colleague getting too stressed or overwhelmed at work, or a neighbor who just lost a loved one, she is always there to help. Jane is also a responsible person who knows how to prioritize her time and beliefs. She is an amazing friend and someone whom I will dearly miss seeing every day at work.*

The Gratitude Statement

Please read Book One of the *Meditations* of Roman Emperor and Stoic philosopher Marcus Aurelius.

Question for you to answer. Following Marcus' general style, please write a concise statement of gratitude identifying the ethical and intellectual debts you owe to family members, teachers, or friends. Fictitious names are permitted, but the statement of gratitude should be genuine.

Comment: *The following observation submitted by an AIS student exemplifies most of the responses we receive:*

> *The format of Marcus Aurelius's statements in his gratitude statement really intrigued me. I think it showed me how grateful I am to have a supporting cast (family, friends, teachers). Additionally, writing the assignment out (with my personal connections) forced me to reflect on my actions and see how much I "cheated myself" out of. I am indebted to all of my close friends, family, and teachers and I owe them to conduct myself in a manner that reflects their honest and generous actions .... I would encourage this sort of reflection activity for others. I feel like from time to time I will do this process to sort out my thoughts and feelings.*

> *Aware only of his own satisfactions and his own happiness, hoarding them as a miser hoards his purse … the egoist cannot be grateful. Ingratitude is not the incapacity to receive but the inability to give back--in the form of joy or love--a little of the joy that was received or experienced. This is why ingratitude is so pervasive a vice. [Ungrateful people] absorb joy as others absorb light, for egoism is a black hole.* [2]
>
> --Andre Comte-Sponville, Professor of philosophy at the Sorbonne (France)

Stories for human connection, ethical development, and self-discovery

The Retirement Banquet and Gratitude Statement exercises invite students to draw upon the human capacity for empathy and social cooperation. Charles Darwin described that capacity as a foundation for ethical development:

> A moral being is one who is capable of reflecting on his past actions and their motives--of approving some and disapproving of others; and the fact that man is the one being who certainly deserves this designation, is the greatest of all distinctions between him and the lower animals . . . . Owing to this condition of mind, man cannot avoid looking both backwards and forwards, and comparing past impressions. Hence, after some temporary desire or passion has mastered his social instincts, he reflects and compares the now weakened expression of such past impulses with the ever-present social instincts; and he then feels that sense of dissatisfaction which all unsatisfied instincts leave behind them, he therefore resolves to act differently for the future,--and this is conscience . . . .

---

2   Andre Comte-Sponville, *A Small Treatise on the Great Virtues* (2002), p.132.

> The appreciation and the bestowal of praise and blame both rest on sympathy; and this emotion, as we have seen, is one of the most important elements of the social instincts. Sympathy, though gained as an instinct, is also much strengthened by exercise or habit . . . . The moral nature of man has reached its present standard, partly through the advancement of his reasoning powers and consequently of a just public opinion, but especially from his sympathies having been rendered more tender and widely diffused through the effects of habit, example, instruction, and reflection.[3]

We examine the connection between social cooperation and the human moral sense throughout this book --citing the work of Martha Nussbaum, Carol S. Dweck, Charles Darwin, E.O. Wilson, Tim Hartford, Robert Sapolsky, Ralph Gomory, Antonio Damasio, and Jonathan Haidt, among others. A genetic predisposition to cooperation, however, isn't a guaranteed pathway to higher forms of ethical development. Environmental influences--including family, peers, and culture--can turn the natural willingness of children to help others into irrational hatred of strangers.

When Darwin wrote that human beings can look both forward and backwards, he was describing our capacity for mental time travel. One evolutionary outcome of this capacity is the construction of an internal narrative (try to imagine yourself without one). Choosing among competing narratives is our biggest challenge. Harriet Beecher Stowe's Uncle Tom's Cabin might have inspired abolitionism in the United States,[4] but the film The Birth of a Nation did the opposite. Advancing

---

3   Darwin, Charles, The Descent of Man, Norton Critical Edition (2001), pp. 200-201.

4   Lincoln himself understood how empathy could be evoked by compelling stories. In 1862, when introduced to Harriet Beecher Stowe (author of Uncle Tom's Cabin), he reportedly made the playful comment "so you're the little woman who wrote the book that started this great war." See Harriet Beecher Stowe: The little woman who wrote the book that started this great war (Ohio State University).

Harvard psychologist Steven Pinker emphasized the role of literature in the expansion of empathy and an overall decline of violence worldwide. The following paragraph from his book The Better Angels of Our Nature: Why Violence Has Declined (2011) contains a concise summary of his thesis:

> [T]echnological advances in publishing, the mass production of books, the expansion of literacy, and the popularity of the novel all preceded the major humanitarian reforms of the 18th century. And in some cases a bestselling novel or memoir demonstrably exposed a wide range of readers to the suffering of a forgotten class of victims and led to a change in policy.

a commitment to more expansive forms of empathy and cooperation requires added components of reason, experience, and knowledge. William Storr wrote in this regard that:

> Story, then, is both tribal propaganda and the cure for tribal propaganda. Atticus Finch, in Harper Lee's To Kill a Mockingbird, advises his daughter that she'll "get along a lot better with all kinds of folks" if she learns a simple trick: "You never really understand a person until you consider things from his point of view . . . until you climb into his skin and walk around in it." This is precisely what story enables us to do. In this way, it creates empathy. There can hardly be a better medicine than that for the groupish hatred that comes so naturally and seductively to all humans.[5]

Stories to enhance engagement in learning

One of the founding stories in western civilization depicts the insatiable curiosity associated with engagement in learning. Why did Odysseus have himself tied to the mast? He insisted on hearing the fateful sirens--while requiring his shipmates to plug their ears. His ultimate goal was to become the first person to *actually listen* to the sirens' songs and live to tell the tale. There are many meanings in this story, but one of the most important is Homer's depiction of a hero as someone who is an *irrepressible learner* as well as a great warrior.

Around the same time that Uncle Tom's Cabin mobilized abolitionist sentiment in the United States, Charles Dickens's Oliver Twist (1838) and Nicholas Nickleby (1839) opened people's eyes to the mistreatment of children in British workhouses and orphanages and Richard Henry Dana's Two Years Before the Mast: A Personal Narrative of Life at Sea (1840) and Herman Melville's White Jacket helped end the flogging of sailors. In the past century Erich Maria Remarque's All Quiet on the Western Front, George Orwell's 1984, Arthur Koestler's Darkness at Noon, Aleksandr Solzhenitsyn's One Day in the Life of Ivan Denisovich, Harper Lee's To Kill a Mockingbird, Elie Wiesel's Night, Kurt Vonnegut's Slaughterhouse- Five, Alex Haley's Roots, Anchee Min's Red Azalea, Azar Nafisi's Reading Lolita in Tehran, and Alice Walker's Possessing the Secret of Joy (a novel that features female genital mutilation) all raised public awareness of the suffering of people who might otherwise have been ignored." See: "Extract: The Better Angels of Our Nature by Steven Pinker" in The Guardian, November 1, 2011.

5   Storr, William, *The Science of Storytelling: Why Stories Make Us Human and How to Tell Them Better* (2020), p. 210.

*The Duke of Sheh asked about Confucius.... The Teacher
[Confucius] said, "Why didn't you just [say] I am a
man who in eagerness for study forgets to eat, in his
enjoyment of it, forgets his problems...."*

--Confucius Analects, 7:19 [6]

Engagement in learning is exemplified in the life example of Abraham Lincoln (also featured in Chapter six and Appendix One). This characteristic can be seen in a statue on the campus of Syracuse University.[7] Lincoln is depicted sitting on a horse stopped to eat grass. A distracted Lincoln--engaged in a book--takes no notice.

Photo by Gary Pavela

The statue is fitting. People who knew Lincoln referred to him as a "stubborn reader." Historian William Lee Miller wrote:

6   Confucius *Analects, 7:19.*

7   AIS document "Abraham Lincoln and Engagement in Learning."

> It would be quite a study to go through the available record to identify all the places, times, and postures in which those who had known Lincoln in Indiana and in New Salem remembered him reading a book: reading while the horse rests at the end of a row, reading while walking down the street, reading under a tree, reading while others went to dances, reading with his legs up as high as his head, reading between customers in the post office, reading snatched at length on the counter of the store.[8]

For all his outward gregariousness, Lincoln was a solitary man who rarely revealed himself to others. Reading was an antidote to loneliness and a way for a precocious mind to find companionship.

Troubled college students sometimes make the mistake of regarding reading and studying as stressful diversions from their inner turmoil. The opposite is true. Few pursuits are more conducive to mental health than engagement in learning.

Perhaps the best way teachers can encourage engagement in learning is to demonstrate it themselves. Do they share Aristotle's view that "to learn gives the liveliest pleasure?" [9] If so, how is that belief demonstrated to students?

Teachers who display their own engagement in learning are sending an implicit message: *they don't know everything.* An admission of incomplete knowledge is an invitation to partnership with students. Both can engage in the pursuit of wisdom together.[10]

---

8   Miller, William Lee, Lincoln's Virtues: An Ethical Biography (2002), p. 48.

9   Aristotle, *Poetics*, Chapter IV (Monadnock Valley Press).

10   Pavela, Gary, "Academic Freedom for Students Has Ancient Roots," *Chronicle of Higher Education,* May 27, 2005. Updated by the author on MEDIUM at https://bit.ly/3xYJas3.

> *Highly effective teachers … often display openness with students and may, from time to time, talk about their own intellectual journey, its ambitions, triumphs, frustrations, and failures, and encourage their students to be similarly reflective and candid. They may discuss how they developed their interests, the major obstacles they faced in mastering the subject, or some of their secrets for learning particular material. They often discuss openly and enthusiastically their own sense of awe and curiosity about life.* [11]
>
> --Ken Bain, *What the Best College Teachers Do*

AIS tutors also suggest to students that building competency in any field doesn't have to entail mindless drudgery. Psychologist Mihaly Csikszentmihalyi cited the example of a "well-known West Coast rock climber" who exhibited characteristics of what Csikszentmihalyi called "flow:"

> It's exhilarating to come closer and closer to self-discipline. You make your body go and everything hurts, then you look back in awe at the self, and what you've done, it just blows your mind. It leads to ecstasy, to self-fulfillment. If you win these battles often enough, that battle against yourself, at least for a moment, it becomes easier to win the battles in the world.

Csikszentmihalyi wrote that "the 'battle' is not really *against* the self, but against the entropy that brings disorder to consciousness" [emphasis in the original]. Those who succeed in this effort, he wrote, will understand that the "deep enjoyment" flow provides "requires an equal degree of disciplined concentration." [12]

---

11   Bain, Ken, *What the Best College Teachers Do* (2004), p. 18.

12   Csikszentmihalyi, Mihaly, *Flow* (1990), pp. 40-41.

Physicist Richard Feynman suggested that deep engagement in learning can also occur--and perhaps be more enduring--when explorers don't have a predetermined objective:

> I think what we're doing is exploring, we're trying to find out as much as we can about the world. People say to me, "Are you looking for the ultimate laws of physics?" No, I'm not, I'm just looking to find out more about the world and if it turns out there is a simple ultimate law which explains everything, so be it, that would be very nice to discover. If it turns out it's like an onion with millions of layers and we're just sick and tired of looking at the layers, then that's the way it is, but whatever way it comes out, nature is there and she's going to come out the way she is, and therefore when we go to investigate it, we shouldn't pre-decide what it is we're trying to do except to try to find out more about it . . . . *My interest in science is to simply find out about the world, and the more I find out the better it is* [emphasis added].[13]

Stories to build a commitment to truth-seeking and truth-telling

Stories taught in the Academic Integrity Seminar encourage students to identify truth-seeking and truth-telling as essential in building an admirable character and a better world. Making such an effort isn't a solitary endeavor. It entails a communal orientation (truth-seeking becomes stunted without collaboration) and a social obligation (lying and deception undermine the trust which makes collaboration possible). It's also important to emphasize that *truth-seeking* is not the same as *ultimate truth-finding*. Too much needless harm and suffering are associated with the latter perspective--grounded (as it typically is) in what Isaiah Berlin described as "unbridled monism" in pursuit of an ever-elusive perfection.[14]

---

13 Feynman, Richard, *The Pleasure of Finding Things Out: The Best Short Works of Richard P. Feynman* (2005), p. 23.

14 Berlin, Isaiah, *The Power of Ideas* (2002), p. 14. Also published in the *New York Review of Books*, Vol. XLV, Number 8 (1998). Berlin wrote:

> The enemy of pluralism is monism -- the ancient belief that there is a single harmony of truths into which everything, if it is genuine, in the end must fit. The consequence of this belief (which is something different from, but akin to, what Karl Popper called essentialism -- to

Most examples of truth-seeking and truth telling in AIS readings are drawn from the methodological tradition of science (also discussed in Chapter Five).[15] One of the most famous defenders of that tradition is the American philosopher John Dewey. He wrote:

> Those . . . who have arrogated to themselves the title of "fundamentalists" recognize no mean between their dogmas and . . . hopeless uncertainty . . . . Until they have been reborn into the life of intelligence, they will not be aware that there are a steadily increasing number of persons who find security in methods of inquiry, of observation, experiment, of forming and following working hypotheses. Such persons are not unsettled by the upsetting of any special belief, because they retain security of procedure. They can say, borrowing language from another context, though this method slay my most cherished belief, yet will I trust it." [16]

It takes a special kind of intellect to see the scientific method as inspirational. College educators might go beyond John Dewey's analytical approach and personalize the *feelings* involved. A good example can be found in Simon Blackburn's review of Richard Dawkins' book *A Devil's Chaplain: Reflections on Hope, Lies, Science, and Love*. Blackburn, professor of philosophy at the University of Cambridge, wrote:

---

him the root of all evil) is that those who know should command those who do not. Those who know the answers to some of the great problems of mankind must be obeyed, for they alone know how society should be organized, how individual lives should be lived, how culture should be developed. This is the old Platonic belief in the philosopher-kings, who were entitled to give orders to others . . . .

Someone once remarked that in the old days men and women were brought as sacrifices to a variety of gods; for these, the modern age has substituted the new idols: isms. To cause pain, to kill, to torture are in general rightly condemned; but if these things are done not for my personal benefit but for an ism -- socialism, nationalism, fascism, communism, fanatically held religious belief, or progress, or the fulfillment of the laws of history -- then they are in order. Most revolutionaries believe, covertly or overtly, that in order to create the ideal world eggs must be broken, otherwise one cannot obtain an omelette. Eggs are certainly broken -- never more violently than in our times -- but the omelette is far to seek, it recedes into an infinite distance. *That is one of the corollaries of unbridled monism, as I call it -- some call it fanaticism, but monism is at the root of every extremism* [emphasis added].

15   See our discussion of the methodology of science in Chapter Five and related footnotes notes therein (especially notes 22-28).

16   Cited in Rockefeller, Steven, *John Dewey: Religious Faith and Democratic Humanism* (1991) pp. 442-443.

Dawkins unashamedly and gloriously delights in science. If anything is sacred to him, it is truth and the patient road to it. He loves the methods of science and its self-correcting nature. He loves the amazing world that it reveals—a world far more amazing than any that human beings could invent out of their own heads. A quotation that he provides from Douglas Adams fits him exactly: "I'd take the awe of understanding over the awe of ignorance any day." [17]

Key words in the preceding paragraph include "awe," "loves," and "amazing"—all associated with the pursuit of truth in the sciences. Those emotions can give meaning to truth-seeking in any discipline and have the added benefit of making academic fraud and dishonesty inherently repugnant.[18]

The sense of responsibility associated with truth-seeking and truth telling in the sciences is demonstrated by a personal example shared with AIS students. The example entails a decision by a courageous graduate student to report a mistake that required retraction of a journal article. The graduate student wrote:

> When I discovered the contamination, I could have quietly moved on and likely nobody would have ever known. Some selfish, anxious part of me wanted to do that. But I believe in the importance of intellectual honesty and owning my mistakes and never seriously flirted with the idea of burying them . . . .

> Here is the silver lining: I learned something, which is what science is about. I learned that the stigma I perceived was predominantly coming from my own ego. I learned how kind people could be about an honest mistake. I did the right thing, and none of the awful consequences I imagined following came to pass . . . . [I]n the end what really matters is

---

17   Cited in Blackburn, Simon, "The Ethics of Belief," *New Republic*, December 1, 2003. An abbreviated reference also appears in Encyclopedia.com at the Richard Dawkins entry.

18   Much of the language in this section comes from our previously published work, including MEDIUM essays by Gary Pavela: "What is Truth? Perspectives from Jerusalem, Rome, and Athens" and "The Meaning of 'Belief + Doubt = Sanity."

the science and getting it as right as possible. Avoid mistakes with careful science. Correct them with honesty and humility. Have some faith that your fellow scientists will understand. And then get back to the lab.[19]

When problems are discovered after publication, retract the paper and do the experiment over… Treasure and support students that show their honesty and conviction when they point out their own mistakes. There should be no shame in an honest retraction, though there will always be regret.

-- Joan E. Strassmann "Retraction with Honor."

Our related MEDIUM essay "Introducing Students to the Aims and Methodology of Science" (online Appendix) contains an assignment related to this topic. AIS tutor comments are included.

Truth-seeking and truth-telling are also associated with unbiased efforts to seek wisdom from diverse sources. AIS tutors cite Nelson Mandela as an aspirational role model in this regard. In his famous "Statement from the Dock at the Opening of the Defense Case in the Rivonia Trial" (April 1964), Mandela said:

[F]rom my reading of Marxist literature and from conversations with Marxists, I have gained the impression that communists regard the parliamentary system of the West as undemocratic and reactionary. But, on the contrary, I am an admirer of such a system.

---

19   Strassmann, Joan E. (research team lead professor), "Retraction with Honor" (Blog).

The Magna Carta, the Petition of Rights, the Bill of Rights are documents which are held in veneration by democrats throughout the world.

I have great respect for British political institutions, and for the country's system of justice. I regard the British Parliament as the most democratic institution in the world, and the independence and impartiality of its judiciary never fail to arouse my admiration.

The American Congress, that country's doctrine of separation of powers, as well as the independence of its judiciary, arouse in me similar sentiments.

I have been influenced in my thinking by both West and East. All this has led me to feel that in my search for a political formula, I should be absolutely impartial and objective. [20]

We urge students to see universities as places where truth-seeking occurs in an atmosphere of intellectual freedom and diversity. A 1995 decision by the United States Supreme Court remains a foundational statement in this regard. Writing for the majority in *Rosenberger v. the Rector and Board of Visitors of the University of Virginia*, Justice Anthony Kennedy stated: "In ancient Athens, and, as Europe entered into a new period of intellectual awakening, in places like Bologna, Oxford, and Paris, universities began as voluntary and spontaneous assemblages or concourses for students to speak and to write and to learn . . . . For the university, by regulation, to cast disapproval on particular viewpoints of its students risks the suppression of free speech and creative inquiry in one of the vital centers for the nation's intellectual life, its college and university campuses." [21]

---

20   Mandela, Nelson, Statement from the Dock (April 1964).

21   *Rosenberger v. the Rector and Board of Visitors of the University of Virginia* 515 U.S. 819. Available online through the Legal Information Institute, Cornell Law School.

> Every intellectual revolution which has ever stirred
> humanity into greatness has been a passionate protest
> against inert ideas. Then, alas, with pathetic ignorance
> of human psychology, it has proceeded by some
> educational scheme to bind humanity afresh with inert
> ideas of its own fashioning. [22]
>
> --Alfred North Whitehead, *The Aims of Education*

Justice Kennedy identified ancient Athens as a place where students were seen as partners in academic life.[23] Teaching in Plato's Academy was a form of soul-craft, based on friendship in pursuit of truth. Indeed, the center of Raphael's famous fresco *The School of Athens*[24] shows Plato, the teacher, pointing up to a vision of eternal harmony, while Aristotle, many years younger and the student, seeks to bring him down to earth to explore and understand the world as it is. Raphael's image depicts what Aristotle described in his *Nicomachean Ethics* as an enduring friendship—even as the two disagreed about fundamental philosophical issues.[25]

"Teaching in Plato's Academy was a form of soul-craft, based on friendship in pursuit of truth."

---

22   Whitehead, Alfred, *The Aims of Education* (1929), p. 2.

23   See Pavela, Gary Student Academic Freedom Has Ancient Roots, *Chronicle of Higher Education* and MEDIUM, January 26, 2002.

24   The School of Athens (Wikimedia, public domain).

25   This discussion is drawn from our May 27, 2005 *Chronicle of Higher Education* essay "Academic freedom for students has ancient roots."

Plato (left) and Aristotle (right) in Raphael's *School of Athens* (public domain)

Stories to demonstrate the importance of trust

In the opening of Chapter Four we contrast two stories referenced in the Academic Integrity Seminar: "The Wolf of Wall Street" (a 2013 film depicting the rise and fall of "financial criminal" [26] Jordan Belfort) with Federal Reserve Board Chair Alan Greenspan's "musings of an old, idealistic, central banker" in his 1999 Harvard Commencement speech.[27] Even students who question Greenspan's libertarian leanings--which were not featured in his Harvard speech-- resonate with his observation that *"[t]he true measure of a career is to be able to be content, even proud, that you succeeded through your own endeavors without leaving a trail of casualties in your wake."*

Most aspects of the Jason Belfort story seem *entirely* composed of "leaving a trail of casualties" in his wake. Here's a typical response AIS tutors use whenever an admirably candid student cites Belfort as an aspirational role model:

---

26   Belfort's Wikipedia entry starts with the line: "American entrepreneur, speaker, author, former stockbroker, and financial criminal."

27   Greenspan, Alan, Remarks by Chairman Alan Greenspan: Commencement address at Harvard University, Cambridge, Massachusetts, June 10, 1999.

Your essay referred to Belfort's "success," but most of us define success as meaning more than conspicuous consumption and relentless pursuit of money. Doesn't success also have something to do with making a constructive contribution to the world and sustaining trusted relationships with family and friends? In the latter context, Belfort doesn't seem successful at all. Consider his reported history of *spousal abuse, child endangerment, betrayal of colleagues*, and *drug addiction*. Someone --in Belfort's words-- who had enough sedatives "running through my circulatory system to sedate Guatemala" isn't a likely model of fulfillment or happiness.[28]

Psychoanalyst and anthropologist Michael Maccoby wrote a book titled *The Gamesman*. The word "Gamesman" was chosen to fit a narcissistic personality in any field or profession who engages in a self-centered, no-holds-barred fight "to get to the top." Maccoby concluded that the end result of this fight was likely to be a solitary life devoid of trust:

> An old and tiring gamesman is a pathetic figure, especially after he has lost a few contests, and with them, his confidence. Once his youth, vigor, and even the thrill of winning are lost, he becomes depressed and goalless, questioning the purpose of his life. No longer energized by the . . . struggle and unable to dedicate himself to something he believes in beyond himself . . . *he finds himself starkly alone. His attitude has kept him from deep friendship and intimacy. Nor has he sufficiently developed abilities that would strengthen the self, so that he might gain satisfaction from understanding (science) or creating (invention, art). Without the thrill of the contest, there is nothing* [emphasis added].[29]

AIS tutors also draw upon practical examples in student life that highlight the importance of trust.[30] Here's one of our comments:

---

28   So, Jimmy "The Real Wolf of Wall Street: Jordan Belfort's Vulgar Memoirs," *The Daily Beast*, July 11, 2017 and Belfort, Jordan, *Catching the Wolf of Wall Street* (2011).

29   Maccoby, Michael, *The Gamesman* (1976), p.111.

30   AIS Tutors often cite the following observation by Albert Camus and suggest that *trust between teammates* is one of the moral principles implicit in sports: *"After many years during which I saw*

Pretend a syllabus in one of your classes states the mid-term examination will be on October 10. Then, at the beginning of class on October 3, the teacher announces "I have good news and bad news: the good news is that I just found a great fare to Cancun! The bad news is I have to leave tomorrow. So, the examination scheduled for October 10 will be administered today. I apologize for any inconvenience, but part of what we do at the University is to help prepare students for the unexpected."

Students are typically appalled by this scenario. It strikes them as an obvious breach of trust. AIS tutors then remind them that the principle of *reciprocity* applies. Teachers trust students to do honest work and feel betrayed when that trust is broken.

The reason I moved the word "trustworthy" to my number one spot [in the retirement banquet exercise] is because of the speech given by Greenspan. In this reading, Greenspan talked about how nothing works without trust, not businesses, relationships, or life. Often, we take trust for granted or we just do not notice it, but it plays a huge role in everything we do each day, and that is why it is my number one.

-- AIS student comment

Stories to promote intellectual humility

Intellectual humility is associated with evidence-based reasoning, self-insight, curiosity, sociability, and an active desire to find and consider alternative perspectives.[31] These characteristics are highlighted in an AIS exercise that starts with this question:

---

many things, what I know most surely about morality and the duty of man I owe to sport . . . . " Cited in "Albert Camus and football," the Camus Society.

31   Leary, Mark "What Does Intellectual Humility Look Like?" *Greater Good Magazine*, November 3, 2021. Leary wrote:

[P]eople high in intellectual humility more carefully consider the evidence on which their beliefs are based, are vigilant to the possibility that they might be incorrect, consider the

What accounts for the success of the Wright brothers in producing "the world's first successful flights of a powered heavier-than-air flying machine?" [32]

The answer includes a *"talent for productive argument"* [33] taught to them by their father, Milton Wright.

Author Ian Leslie provided the following background, based on a history by Tom Crouch: [34]

> Milton Wright . . . taught [the brothers] how to argue productively. After the evening meal, Milton would introduce a topic and instruct the boys to debate it as vigorously as possible without being disrespectful. Then he would tell them to change sides and start again. It proved great training.[35]

Arguments between the Wright brothers could become heated ("a good scrap").[36] Crouch, author of the *Bishop's Boys* (1989), wrote that "[i]n time, [the boys] would learn to argue in a more effective way, tossing ideas back and forth in a kind of verbal shorthand until a kernel of truth began to emerge." [37] The end result was summarized by Wilbur Wright:

> *No truth is without some mixture of error, and no error so false that it possesses no element of truth . . . . Honest argument is*

---

perspectives of other informed people (including those whose viewpoints differ from theirs), and revise their views when evidence warrants.

The authors of the Constitution showed a comparable sensibility, demonstrated by their decision to create a mechanism for future amendments.

32   The description is provided by the Smithsonian Institution at http://bit.ly/3o6A0rm ("1903 Wright Flyer").

33   Leslie, Ian, "A Good Scrap: Disagreements Can Be Unpleasant, Even Offensive, but they Are Vital to Human Reason." *Aeon*, July 12, 2021.

34   Crouch, Tom, *The Bishop's Boys: A Life of Wilbur and Orville Wright* (2003).

35   Leslie, Ian, "A Good Scrap: Disagreements Can Be Unpleasant, Even Offensive, but they Are Vital to Human Reason." *Aeon*, July 12, 2021.

36   Leslie, Ian, "A Good Scrap: Disagreements Can Be Unpleasant, Even Offensive, but they Are Vital to Human Reason." *Aeon*, July 12, 2021. Leslie wrote:

> Charles Taylor, who worked on the shop floor of the Wright Cycle Company, described the room above as "frightened with argument." He recalled: "The boys were working out a lot of theory in those days, and occasionally they would get into terrific arguments. They'd shout at each other something terrible. I don't think they really got mad, but they sure got awfully hot."

37   Crouch, Tom, The Bishop's Boys: A Life of Wilbur and Orville Wright (2003), p.103.

merely a process of mutually picking the beams and motes out of each other's eyes so both can see clearly. [38]

We share this story with AIS students because it provides a memorable example of what intellectual humility and respectful dialogue can achieve.

[T]he very essence of modern science is that, having admitted ignorance, we can acquire new knowledge. [39]

--Thomas Hertog, *The Origin of Time: Stephen Hawking's Final Theory*

President Obama introduced the subject of vigorous debate and intellectual humility in his 2016 Commencement address at Rutgers University.

> If you disagree with somebody, bring them in—and ask them tough questions . . . . If somebody has got a bad or offensive idea, prove it wrong. Engage it. Debate it. Stand up for what you believe in . . . . Don't feel like you got to shut your ears off because you're too fragile and somebody might offend your sensibilities. Go at them if they're not making any sense. Use your logic and reason and words. And by doing so, you'll strengthen your own position, and you'll hone your arguments. *And maybe you'll learn something and realize you don't know everything.* And you may have a new understanding not only about what your opponents believe but maybe what you believe. Either way, you win. And more importantly, our democracy wins [emphasis added]. [40]

Praise for intellectual humility (expressed in theory, if not always in practice) is associated with the Socratic tradition--most notably Plato's dialogues *Gorgias, Phaedrus, and The Republic.* Plato's aim

---

38   Tobin, James, *To Conquer the Air* (2004), p. 90.

39   Hertog, Thomas, *On the Origin of Time: Stephen Hawking's Final Theory* (2023), p. 10.

40   Obama, Barack, 2016 commencement speech given at Rutgers University.

in this regard was to distinguish between *rhetoric* (which he saw primarily as the unprincipled pursuit of power) and *dialogue* (the mutual pursuit of wisdom grounded on respectful refutation, similar to Wilbur Wright's argumentation with his brother). James Boyd White (Emeritus Professor of Law at the University of Michigan) provided a description of this process in a classic *University of Chicago Law Review* article sometimes shared with AIS students: "[R]hetoric naturally treats others as means to an end, while dialectic treats others as ends in themselves . . . . This is not a competition to see who can reduce the other to his will, but mutual discovery by mutual refutation . . . . The object of it all is truth, and its method is friendship.[41]

Learning is hard—and it begins with a perception of the self that does not sit well with self-love. To learn, we have to accept that we are ignorant. There is much we do not know. We are partial, incomplete. It's even possible that much of what we claim to know is not so. We have been duped before, and we no doubt can be again.[42]

--Mark Edmundson, University Professor
of English at the University of Virginia

Mutual learning through respectful dialogue requires cognitive conditioning and disciplined information processing.[43] Do we filter and synthesize knowledge based on whether it matches our assumptions,

---

41   White, James, "The Ethics of Argument: Plato's *Gorgias* and the Modern Lawyer," 50 *University of Chicago Law Review* 849, 870-871, (1983). White wrote:

> [R]hetoric naturally treats others as means to an end, while dialectic treats others as ends in themselves. Rhetoric persuades another not by refuting, but by flattering him, by appealing to what pleases, rather than to what is best for him . . . . Dialectic is wholly different both in method and object. It proceeds not by making lengthy statements . . . but by questioning and answering in one-to-one conversation. Its object is to engage each person at the deepest level, and for this it requires utter frankness of speech on each side . . . . This is not a competition to see who can reduce the other to his will, but mutual discovery by mutual refutation . . . . *The object of it all is truth, and its method is friendship* [emphasis added].

42   Edmundson, Mark, *The Age of Guilt: The Super-Ego in the Online World* (2023), p. 87.

43   See, generally, Leary, Mark *The Psychology of Intellectual Humility* (2018).

or do we seek alternative perspectives that may change what we believe? AIS tutors engage students on this topic by asking them to consider Charles Darwin's "Golden Rule:"

> I had . . . during many years followed a golden rule, namely, that whenever a published fact, a new observation or thought came across me, which was opposed to my general results, to make a memorandum of it without fail and at once; for I had found by experience that such facts and thoughts were far more apt to escape from the memory than favorable ones. Owing to this habit, very few objections were raised against my views which I had not at least noticed and attempted to answer. [44]

The thinking error Darwin was trying to avoid entails repressing or denying contrary arguments. We invite students to consider better alternatives grounded on a capacity to see a "rich, nuanced reality that defies simple mental compartmentalization." [45]

This seminar has taught me the values of being trustworthy and honest and has stressed to me the fact that being these things is the only way to truly be proud of my accomplishments ... If I did not do something to my full ability, what is there to be proud of?

--AIS student comment

---

44   Darwin, Charles *Life and Letters*, Part 1 (1887), p. 36.

45   Alison, Scott, "Heroes: What They Do and Why We Need Them" (Blog post) January 23, 2020. Alison wrote:

> In contrast to dualistic thinking, nondualistic thinking resists a simple definition. It sees subtleties, exceptions, mystery, and a bigger picture. Nondualistic thinking refers to a broader, dynamic, imaginative, and more mature contemplation of perceived events (Rohr, 2009). A nondualistic approach to understanding reality is open and patient with mystery and ambiguity. Nondualistic thinkers see reality clearly because they do not allow their prior beliefs, expectations, and biases to affect their conscious perception of events and encounters with people . . . . Abraham Heschel (1955) described it as the ability to *let the world come at us* rather than *us come at the world* with preconceived categories that can skew our perceptions. "Our goal should be to live life in radical amazement," wrote Heschel. "Wonder or radical amazement, the state of maladjustment to words and notions, is therefore a prerequisite for *an authentic awareness of that which is* " [citation omitted].

We willingly allow highly simplistic narratives to deceive us, gleefully accepting as truth any tale that casts us as the moral hero and the other as the two-dimensional villain. We can tell when we're under its power. When all the good is on our side and all the bad on theirs, our storytelling brain is working its grim magic in full. We're being sold a story. Reality is rarely so simple. Such stories are seductive because our hero-making cognition is determined to convince us of our moral worth. They justify our primitive tribal impulses and seduce us into believing that, even in our hatred, we are holy. [46]

    -- Will Storr, author of *The Science of Storytelling: Why Stories Make Us Human and How to Tell Them Better*

I completed the academic integrity seminar last month and I just wanted to reach out and express how much it has impacted me. I really did not expect to be so affected by it as I had thought my mistake was not a reflection of who I am as a person, but this seminar really opened my eyes to the areas of character that I need to work on. I learned so much from it and just wanted to say thank you.

    --AIS student comment

---

46   Storr, Will, *The Science of Storytelling: Why Stories Make Us Human and How to Tell Them Better* (2020), p. 162.

AIS SAMPLE EXERCISE

One of our most appreciated assignments focuses on the life and work of Frederick Douglass--especially his relationship with Abraham Lincoln.

Please read and consider these two speeches by Frederick Douglass:

The Composite Nation (1869; excerpts) [47]

Oration in Memory of Abraham Lincoln (1876; excerpts) [48]

Two questions for you to answer (based on your reading of both speeches):

[1] What qualities does Douglass display *as a thinker* and *a writer*? People continue to read these speeches because they're powerful and memorable. What *makes* them powerful and memorable? Cite a specific example from the speeches to support your answer.

[2] What *qualities of character* does Douglass display in these speeches? That is, what do you find memorable about Douglass as a person, based on *what* he wrote and *how* he expressed himself? Cite a specific example from the speeches to support your answer.

---

47   Douglass, Frederick, "A Composite Nation" (1867). Available on the "Black Past" website.

48   Douglass, Frederick, "Oration in Memory of Abraham Lincoln" (1876).

The following AIS tutor comment emphasizes Douglass's capacity for candid analysis:

In theory and practice, Douglass lived a life of integrity. Truth-telling and intellectual honesty were essential to his persuasive power. In his Eulogy for Abraham Lincoln, for example, Douglass refused to see Lincoln simplistically--either as a saint or a hypocrite. Truth-telling meant highlighting Lincoln's slow progress in overcoming racial bigotry; the unique set of challenges he faced in forging the war effort; and the fundamental goodness of his heart ("though Mr. Lincoln shared the prejudices of his white fellow-countrymen against the Negro, it is hardly necessary to say that in his heart of hearts he loathed and hated slavery"). That kind of balanced thinking is hard to find. We tend to think dualistically--"Right vs Wrong"--even when we know truth is rarely seen and explained so easily.

I really admire Douglass for being critical yet so analytical of another person where he considered both the positive and negative sides to Lincoln. I aspire to be this way, and it is a big reason why my five [self] descriptive words changed immensely.

-- AIS student comment

Frederick Douglass was adept at recognizing the multiple challenges Lincoln faced before and during the civil war. "Had he put the abolition of slavery before the salvation of the Union," Douglass said, "he would have inevitably driven from him a powerful class of the American people and rendered resistance to rebellion impossible." [49] In this context, Douglass was analyzing the conduct of the war *from Lincoln's perspective.* By doing so (while freely voicing his own disagreement), Douglass allowed other observers to come closer to a multifaceted view of Lincoln's character and personality.

Douglass also described a disagreement with Lincoln during the course of the war about how to retaliate for Confederate mistreatment of captured black soldiers:

> Feeling myself now perfectly free to say to Mr. Lincoln all that I thought on the subject, I supported my demands as best I could with arguments, to which he calmly and patiently listened, not once interrupting me . . . and when I had finished he made a careful reply, covering each proposition that I had submitted to him.

> [W]hen it came to the matter of retaliation, the tender heart of the president appeared in the expression of his eyes, and in every line of his care worn countenance, as well as in the tones of his appealing voice. "Ah!" said he, "Douglass, I cannot hang men in cold blood. I cannot hang men who have had nothing

---

49　Douglass, Frederick, "Oration in Memory of Abraham Lincoln" (1876).

to do with murdering colored prisoners. Of course, if I could get hold of the actual murderers of colored prisoners I would deal with them as they deserve, but I cannot hang those who had no hand in such murders." I was not convinced that Mr. Lincoln himself was right. I could, and did, answer [his] arguments; but was silenced by his over-mastering mercy and benevolence. I had found a president with a heart — one who could, even in war, love his enemies; and that was something. In parting he said: "Douglass, never come to Washington without calling upon me." And I never did. [50]

Lincoln and Douglass grew to admire each other[51] in part because candid and respectful disagreements allowed them to see each other whole.[52] The implications go beyond the lives of two extraordinary

---

50   Hord, Fred Lee and Norman, Matthew, Ed., *Knowing Him By Heart: African-Americans on Abraham Lincoln* (2022), p. 403.

51   Stauffer, John, *Giants: The Parallel Lives of Frederick Douglass and Abraham Lincoln* (2009), Kindle location 50. Stauffer is Chair of the History of American Civilization and Professor of English and African and African American Studies at Harvard University. He said in a 2008 interview:

> Douglass and Lincoln were pragmatists, able to put aside their vast differences and come together as friends. In 1860 Douglass helped elect Lincoln as president. At a time when most whites would not let a black man cross their threshold, Lincoln met Douglass three times at the White House. Their friendship was chiefly utilitarian: Lincoln needed Douglass to help him destroy the Confederacy; Douglass knew that Lincoln could help him end slavery. But they also genuinely liked and admired each other. Douglass and Lincoln ultimately understood that continual self-making was antithetical to racism. This was because the idea of "whiteness" as a sign of superiority depended on a self that was fixed and unchanging. They stood at the forefront of a major shift in cultural history, which rejected fixed social stations and included blacks and whites, though rarely women, in the national ideals of freedom and equality.

Frederick Douglass's assessment of Lincoln's character captures critical aspects of emotional intelligence. In his April 14, 1876 "Oration in Memory of Abraham Lincoln," Douglass said:

> His personal traits and public acts are better known to the American people than are those of any other man of his age. He was a mystery to no man who saw him and heard him. Though high in position, the humblest could approach him and feel at home in his presence. Though deep, he was transparent; though strong, he was gentle; though decided and pronounced in his convictions, he was tolerant toward those who differed from him, and patient under reproaches. Even those who only knew him through his public utterance obtained a tolerable clear idea of his character and his personality. The image of the man went out with his words, and those who read them, knew him.

52   See Ian, Leslie, *Conflicted: How Constructive Disagreements Lead to Better Outcomes* (2021). Leslie wrote:

> We don't just do our thinking 'in the brain,' however. We do it with each other. Our focus on individuals means we underrate disagreement as a route to insight . . . .

> Scientists who study group decision-making . . . have observed ways in which the absence of disagreement within a group of intelligent people can lead to bad decisions. The better known one is driven by the desire to conform, to follow the lead of a dominant person or people in the room. . . . The social psychologist Irving Janis, the first to name this phenomenon, in

individuals to encompass the nature of successful learning and the foundation of a democratic society.

Douglass and Lincoln ultimately understood that continual self-making was antithetical to racism. This was because the idea of "whiteness" as a sign of superiority depended on a self that was fixed and unchanging. They stood at the forefront of a major shift in cultural history ....[53]

-- John Stauffer, Chair of the History of American Civilization and Professor of English and African and African American Studies at Harvard University.

Overall, we encourage AIS students to understand that intellectual humility is a quality of emotional intelligence that expands knowledge,[54] enhances cognitive capacity, promotes cooperation, and inhibits our recurring tendency to perceive unquestionable truth as a component of personal or tribal identity. Whatever may be lost by forgoing *absolute certainty* will be surpassed by an expanded capacity for *cooperation, creativity, and wonder* that benefits us all. See our related MEDIUM essay "The Meaning of 'Belief + Doubt = Sanity'" in the Appendix.

1972, called it "group-think." The problem here, you might say, is that the group acts like an impulsive individual, p. 52.

53   Stauffer, John, Giants: The Parallel Lives of Frederick Douglass and Abraham Lincoln (2009), Kindle location, 78. See note 52 here.

54   The expansion of knowledge occurs, in part, by exploring different depictions of reality. See an observation by Gary Pavela in the April 18, 2003 issue of *The Chronicle of Higher Education*. Pavela wrote:

> In my senior-level seminar on historiography, I encountered this observation from the Oxford philosopher W. H. Walsh in his book *An Introduction to Philosophy of History* (1951), p. 113:
>
> > Just as a portrait painter sees his subject from his own peculiar point of view, but would nevertheless be said to have some insight into that subject's 'real' nature, so too the historian must look at the past with his own presuppositions, but is not thereby cut off from all understanding of it.
>
> For me, Walsh's "portrait painter" metaphor has been an invaluable guide through the intellectual world of the past 40 years. Truth, to some extent, is culturally defined, and remains elusive. But cynicism about seeing or defining *any* aspect of truth is one of the great (and inherently self-contradictory) falsehoods of our time.

The spirit of liberty is the spirit which is not too sure that it is right.... [55]

--Judge Learned Hand, 1944 address
in New York's Central Park

Stories to enhance courage, integrity, and resilience

Part of the universal appeal of stories is the struggle of protagonists to overcome setbacks and challenges. Even when they don't succeed, we want to see how they react. What lessons did they learn? What qualities of character did they display? How might they be worthy of emulation? If these questions sound vaguely familiar, it's because they arise from archetypal hero myths worldwide.

New York Times columnist David Brooks wrote that Robert Kennedy, "devoured by grief " after the assassination of his brother, turned to a book given to him by Jackie Kennedy, *The Greek Way* [56] by Edith Hamilton. Brooks wrote that Kennedy memorized a passage from Aeschylus, which Hamilton quoted twice in her book:

> God, whose law it is that he who learns must suffer. And even in our sleep pain that cannot forget, falls drop by drop upon the heart, and in our own despair, against our will, comes wisdom . . . . [57]

Brooks concluded that:

> If they were doctors of the spirit, the Greeks' specialty was to take grief and turn it into resolution . . . . The story of Kennedy's grief is the story of a man stepping out of his time and fetching from the past a sturdier ethic . . . . The leaders who founded the country were steeped in the classics;

---

55   Hand, Learned (1872-1961); United States Court of Appeals for the Second Circuit) cited in Smith, D. Brooks, *"Learned Hand's Spirit of Liberty: A Lesson for Our Times"* Duke University Law School (2021).

56   Hamilton, Edith, *The Greek Way* (2010).

57   "Aeschylus," Oxford Essential Quotations, 5th ed. (2017).

Kennedy found them in crisis, and today's students are lucky if they stumble on them by happenstance.[58]

Aristotle made recovery from failure a component of his philosophy. AIS students are frequently introduced to this passage in his Nicomachean Ethics:

> Now many events happen by chance . . .[some will] turn out ill [and] crush and maim happiness; for they both bring pain with them and hinder many activities. Yet even in these nobility shines through, when a man bears with resignation many great misfortunes, not through insensibility to pain but through nobility and greatness of soul . . . . For the man who is truly good and wise, we think, bears all the chances [in] life becomingly and always makes the best of circumstances, as a good general makes the best military use of the army at his command [even after a defeat] and a good shoemaker makes the best shoes out of the hides that are given him; and so with all other craftsmen . . . .[59]

For a visual depiction of the Hellenistic view of nobility "shining through" suffering, see what the *Wall Street Journal* calls "one of the most moving works of art ever made." This statue, likely created between 350 and 50 BC, shows a seated boxer "after a bruising bout it is hardly clear he has won . . . [a]nd given the pugilistic conventions of the ancient world, he may be called upon to rise again at any moment to encounter yet another opponent." [60]

---

58   Brooks, David, "The Education of Robert Kennedy," November 26, 2006, *New York Times*.

59   Aristotle, *Nicomachean Ethics* (Book I, 10).

60   Gardner, James, "Masterpiece: Boxer at Rest" *Wall Street Journal*, June 14, 2013.

"Boxer at Rest" Public domain

*It is not doctrines that console us in the end, but people:
their singularity, their courage and steadfastness…
people [who] show us what it means to go on, to keep
going, despite everything.* [61]
-- Michael Ignatieff, *On Finding Consolation in Dark Times*

Telling evocative stories to foster resilience is also a component of contemporary psychological research and writing. One of the best known practitioners of that art was psychiatrist Oliver Sacks. In a review of John Hull's book *Touching the Rock,* Sacks wrote that Hull— who was totally blind—was able to find:

---

61   Ignatieff, Michael, *On Consolation: Finding Solace in Dark Times* (2021), p. 258. See the related National Library of Medicine review.

a new organization and depth and identity. After sinking hopelessly into a bottomless ocean, he discover[ed], in his deepest depths, his anchor and soul: this, for [him], [was] 'touching the rock.' [62]

Students with mood disorders can encounter a level of depression and suicidality that requires prompt mental health intervention. [63] With appropriate support and treatment, "touching the rock" may then allow them to exhibit insight and comprehension that can enrich everyone they know.[64]

AIS students are introduced to the life and work of psychiatrist Roberto Assagioli. He's featured in Chapter Three. Assagioli's description of "disidentification and identification" [65] helps students visualize what *touching the rock* might mean for them.

---

62   Sacks, Oliver, "The 'Dark, Paradoxical Gift'", *New York Review of Books*, April 11, 1991. Full passage:

> "Being a W[hole] B[ody] S[eer]," he writes in his postscript, "is to be in one of the concentrated human conditions. It is a state, like the state of being young, or of being old, of being male or female; it is one of the orders of human being." And in the completeness of this state—which reminds one somewhat of the completeness of "deep deafness" described by the poet David Wright in his book Deafness—there is a new organization and depth and identity. After sinking hopelessly into a bottomless ocean, he discovers, in his deepest depths, his anchor and soul: this, for Hull, is "touching the rock."

63   Richtel, Matt "'It's Life or Death': The Mental Health Crisis Among U.S. Teens," *New York Times*, April 23, 2022. Here's relevant guidance we share with AIS students:

Be wary of thinking disorders that promote self-defeating pessimism. You probably remember this passage written by Abraham Lincoln when he was a young adult (cited in The Atlantic article we assigned):

> *"I am now the most miserable man living. If what I feel were equally distributed to the whole human family, there would not be one cheerful face on the earth … Whether I shall ever be better I can not tell; I awfully forebode I shall not."*

William James (seen as the "father of American psychology") wrote something similar when he was in his twenties:

> *"I am a low-lived wretch. I've been prey to such disgust for life during the past three months as to make letter writing almost an impossibility."*

William James, like Abraham Lincoln, encountered bouts of depression. Each in their own way *sought help* for what they recognized could be debilitating mood disorders. That help—even more readily available now from mental health professionals—enabled them to pass through the storms of early adulthood to *create a sense of purpose* that defined them and enriched the world.

64   See Pavela, Gary, "Fearing Our Students Won't Help Them," *Chronicle of Higher Education*, February 18, 2008.

65   Keen, Sam, "The Golden Mean of Roberto Assagioli", *Psychology Today*, December, 1974.

> Often a crisis in life deprives a person of the function or role with which he has identified: an athlete's body is maimed, a lover's beloved departs with a wandering poet; a dedicated worker must retire. Then the process of disidentification is forced on one and a solution can only come by a process of death and rebirth in which the person enters into a broader identity. But this process can occur with conscious cooperation.

> *The reading that stuck with me the most was the section on Assagioli, particularly the quote: "I have a body, but I am not my body. I have emotions, but I am not my emotions. I have a job, but I am not my job …." It reminded me that I am not only made up of my mistakes. It is possible for me to change and become better and that part in the reading brought a sort of calm feeling to me. It was a reminder that I really needed.*
>
> *--AIS student comment*

How else can lives be enriched by narrative? Psychiatrist and Pulitzer Prize-winning author Robert Coles titled one of his books "*The Call of Stories: Teaching and the Moral Imagination*." [66] His insights include the observation that mental health professionals and teachers must engage in both storytelling and *"story-listening*." In that context, students in AIS tutorials know that someone is reading what they write. They then become teachers themselves. The impact is even greater when a supportive reader/teacher responds with candid commentary, sometimes derived from their own life experience.

The capacity of stories to enhance resilience is not grounded on depictions of perfection. As Will Storr observed, the most consequential stories invite us to "enter the flawed mind of another" and be "reassured that it's not only us" who sometimes feel "confused" or "broken." [67] In this context, providing young people with the right stories may be the most valuable resource educators can give students encountering the challenges of adulthood.

[An] exercise in disidentification and identification involves practicing awareness and affirming: I have a body, but I am not my body. *I have emotions, but I am not my emotions.* I have a job, but I am not my job... etc. Systematic introspection can help to eliminate all partial self-identifications [emphasis added].

66   Coles, Robert, *The Call of Stories: Teaching and the Moral Imagination* (2014).

67   Storr, Will, *The Science of Storytelling* (2020), p. 211.

CHAPTER TWO

GRATITUDE

Marcus Aurelius wrote his famous gratitude statement in times not unlike our own. He faced revolts, invasions, multiple deaths of friends and family, and the Antonine Plague of 165 to 180 AD--which ultimately caused his death and the death of millions of people throughout the Roman empire. Even in this context, expressing gratitude wasn't a burden. Doing so allowed Marcus to reiterate a fundamental lesson in Stoicism and contemporary cognitive behavioral therapy: We have at least some control over the focus of our attention. Shall we dwell among thoughts about a dreadful past or a frightening future, or should we concentrate on the beauty, goodness, and love we experience now?

-- authors of Driving Plato's Chariot

The Gratitude statement of Marcus Aurelius

One of the world's most famous gratitude statements was written by Roman Emperor and Stoic philosopher Marcus Aurelius (121-180 AD).[1] This was the story of Marcus's personal development in relationship with friends, family and mentors.

Here's an excerpt:

> **From my grandfather Verus** I learned good morals and the government of my temper.

---

1   Aurelius, Marcus, *Meditations* (167 ACE), translated by George Long.

From the reputation and remembrance of my father, modesty and a manly character.

From my mother, piety and beneficence, and abstinence, not only from evil deeds, but even from evil thoughts; and further, simplicity in my way of living, far removed from the habits of the rich . . . .

From my governor, to be neither of the green nor of the blue party at the games in the Circus . . . from him too I learned endurance of labor, and to want little, and to work with my own hands, and not to meddle with other people's affairs, and not to be ready to listen to slander.

From Diognetus, not to busy myself about trifling things, and not to give credit to what was said by miracle-workers and jugglers about incantations and the driving away of daemons and such things; and not to breed quails for fighting . . . and to endure freedom of speech; and to have become intimate with philosophy . . . .

From Rusticus, I received the impression that my character required improvement and discipline; and from him I learned to write my letters with . . . respect to those who have offended me by words, or done me wrong, to be easily disposed to be pacified and reconciled, as soon as they have shown a readiness to be reconciled; and to read carefully, and not to be satisfied with a superficial understanding of a book . . . and I am indebted to him for being acquainted with the discourses of Epictetus, which he communicated to me out of his own collection.

Most scholars agree Marcus never intended for his *Meditations* to be read by others. Why, then, did he write them?

Marcus likely found the process of writing the Meditations engaging and reassuring. Doing so was a beautiful act in itself. He also sought insight from the remembrance of people he admired. These are benefits contemporary students can discover as well.

I am grateful, not in order that my neighbor, provoked by the earlier act of kindness, may be more ready to benefit me, but simply in order that I may perform a most pleasant and beautiful act; I feel grateful, not because it profits me, but because it pleases me. [2]

--Seneca, Moral letters to Lucilius

Gratitude as a core human capacity

Yale University President Peter Salovey told graduating students in a 2014 baccalaureate address that "[m]any philosophers—from Cicero to Seneca to Aquinas to Spinoza to Hobbs to Hume and Kant—acknowledge that an ability to express gratitude is not just socially polite but also a core human capacity." [3]

The centrality of gratitude is grounded on the fact that human beings are both *social* and *purpose-driven* animals. As psychologist Robert Emmons suggested in his definition of gratitude, we affirm "that there are good things in the world" and the "sources of this goodness [are] outside of ourselves"--including "other people who . . . gave us many gifts, big and small, to help us achieve the goodness in our lives."[4]

Other people's moral beauty can become a moral compass in our own lives. [5]

-- Dacher Keltner, author of Awe: The New Science of Everyday Wonder and How It Can Transform Your Life

---

2   Seneca (4 BC – AD 65), Moral letters to Lucilius, Letter 81.

3   Salovey, Peter, 2014 Baccalaureate Address at Yale University.

4   Emmons, Robert, "Thanks: How Practicing Gratitude Can Make you Happier" (2007), p. 11.

5   Keltner, Dacher, *Awe: The New Science of Everyday Wonder and How It Can Transform Your Life* (2023), p. 239.

French philosopher Andre Comte-Sponville emphasized this perspective in his book *A Small Treatise on the Great Virtues*:

> Aware only of his own satisfactions and his own happiness, hoarding them as a miser hoards his coin . . . the egoist cannot be grateful. Ingratitude is not the incapacity to receive but the inability to give back--in the form of joy or love--a little of the joy that was received or experienced. This is why ingratitude is so pervasive a vice. [Ungrateful people] absorb joy as others absorb light, for egoism is a black hole.[6]

Fostering grateful minds in schools and colleges

Expressing gratitude allows people to recognize relationships or purposes greater than themselves. You can see this characteristic in the sample exercise on the next page.

Writing the gratitude statement helped me realize what integrity means to me. Far from an abstract concept, it became the one quality that the people I respect the most - my grandmother and parents - have always exemplified. Their integrity makes up who they are.

--AIS student comment

---

6   Comte-Sponville, Andre, *A Small Treatise on the Great Virtues* (2002), p. 134.

AIS SAMPLE EXERCISE

Please read *Book One* [7] of the *Meditations* of Roman Emperor and Stoic philosopher Marcus Aurelius. (Book One is Marcus' statement of gratitude to family, friends and teachers). *Then write a concise statement of gratitude identifying the ethical and intellectual debts you owe to others. Fictitious names are permitted, but the statement of gratitude should be genuine.*

Comment: the following answers from a group of university undergraduates in a traditional classroom [8] are shared with permission:

> *"From my mother I picked up a curiosity toward the world that knows no bounds, questioning everything I have come to know in an eternal pursuit of truth."*

> *"To my grandmother, I thank her for instilling in me the idea that collections of imperfections make a person. She has taught me the mistakes I have made should not be regrets because you cannot change what happened in the past; you can only define how it will change you in the future."*

> *"I thank my parents for investing almost all their time and energy in the undoubtedly arduous process of bringing me up to the point where I am now. For the countless afternoons spent keeping me focused on books and math problems against the strongest protests a 5 year old could muster, to checking upon me and encouraging me to carry on even after my normally stubborn mind had been considering the impending defeat at the hands of*

---

[7]   Aurelius, Marcus, *Meditations*, Book One (George Long trans.) (republished September 9, 2021).

[8]   This honors seminar was taught by Gary Pavela in a traditional classroom at Syracuse University.

econometrics … I am grateful. The list is far longer and will undoubtedly continue to grow, and so, to summarize: to my parents, thank you."

"[My friend] X's deep sense of loyalty has helped me become a better friend. Our opposite personalities only made our friendship more interesting. Without her I never would have learned the value of having someone in my life who is so different from me …. I am grateful to Y for showing me that people are much more complicated than they first appear. The true person only emerges when another person opens up to them."

"From my grandfather I learned the value of hard work; that we all make mistakes yet the morality of man cannot be judged by singular actions; to continue my education and expand my mind every day" From my dog L, the definition of unconditional love and the value of a sixty second memory."

"My father gave me an unbridled love of knowledge of any kind and the drive to pursue it."

"From my friend C, that finding one's identity as a good friend to others can be a satisfying way to lead life."

Students were subsequently asked if they had sent their statement of gratitude to friends or family. About a third reported doing so. One young woman volunteered that she received a return phone call from her father after he read her paper. He was deeply touched, she said, and *"I think this was the first time I heard him cry."*

> [T]he instinct of imitation is implanted in man from childhood, one difference between him and other animals being that he is the most imitative of living creatures, and through imitation learns his earliest lessons; and no less universal is the pleasure felt in things imitated. [9]
>
> -- Aristotle, *Poetics*

The immediate impact of expressing gratitude

Gratitude statements typically inspire emotional commitment from those who *express* gratitude as well as those who receive it. Pertinent research was summarized by Robert Emmons:

> Our . . . research has shown that grateful people experience higher levels of positive emotions such as joy, enthusiasm, love, happiness, and optimism, and that the practice of gratitude as a discipline protects a person from the destructive impulses of envy, resentment, greed, and bitterness. We have discovered that a person who experiences gratitude is able to cope more effectively with everyday stress, may show increased resilience in the face of trauma-induced stress, and may recover more quickly from illness and benefit from greater physical health. [10]

It's easy to replicate this finding. Write a favorable review about some service you received. Mention the name of a person you'd like to compliment. As you post the review, think about the good feelings you hope to create, both in that person and among their friends, colleagues, and family members.

Now, look inward for a moment. What are *you* feeling as you contemplate what the recipient and other readers will likely experience? Do words like "caring," "sympathetic," or even "joyful" come to mind?

---

9   Aristotle, *Poetics*, Chapter IV (Monadnock Valley Press website).

10   Emmons, Robert, *Thanks: How Practicing Gratitude Can Make you Happier* (2008), p. 11.

Gratitude statements as instructional meditation

Philosopher Pierre Hadot suggested that classical philosophy encompassed spiritual practices[11] designed to help adherents overcome destructive emotions and acquisitive appetites to see a majestic pattern of reason or "Logos" that pervades the universe. One such practice was to study the life and teachings of great sages. Three sayings attributed to the Seven Sages of Greece inscribed on the Temple of Delphi are "Nothing to Excess," "Know Thyself," and "Certainty Brings Ruin"[12] (also referenced in Chapter Three). If we consider these maxims as timely reminders or mantras about how to lead a better life and relate them to individuals Marcus Aurelius praised in his gratitude statement we are entering into a realm that unites aspects of philosophy and religion.

One scholar of Stoicism and cognitive behavioral therapy has observed that "[t]here are some striking passages in *The Meditations* in which Marcus appears to exhibit a painter's eye for visual details like the cracks on a loaf of bread." [13] More may be involved here than Marcus's early training in art. His close attention to visual details [14] is also associated with intense focus or flow. In his book *Flow: The Psychology of Optimal Experience* (1990), psychologist Mihaly Csikszentmihalyi described the phenomenon as a form of "rapt concentration" that can produce both "deep enjoyment" and personal fulfillment.[15]

---

11 Hadot, Pierre, *The Selected Writings of Pierre Hadot: Philosophy as Practice (Re-inventing Philosophy as a Way of Life)* (2020), p. 8.

12 See "The 3 Delphic Maxims" at https://disordersofmood.com/delphic.php.

13 Robertson, Donald, *How to Think Like a Roman Emperor: The Stoic Philosophy of Marcus Aurelius*, (2019), p. 52.

14 In *Book III* of his *Meditations* (MIT Internet Classics Archive, George Long, trans.) Marcus wrote:

> [N]othing is so productive of elevation of mind as to be able to examine methodically and truly every object which is presented to thee in life, and always to look at things so as to see at the same time what kind of universe this is, and what kind of use everything performs in it, and what value everything has with reference to the whole . . . .

> In those words, Marcus described the intense focus of flow ("examine methodically and truly every object") and related it to his belief in a rational order that pervades the universe. He then turned theory into practice by *writing* about his observations in the *Meditations*. He realized in this regard that writing is distilled thinking. Given a proper subject, such as admirable qualities of character in others, writing can engage a portion of the brain that fosters emotional intelligence.

15 Csikszentmihalyi, Mihaly, *Flow* (1990), pp. 46-47 and 40-41.

Wallace Stevens provided an unforgettable interpretation of flow in his poem "The House Was Quiet and The World was Calm" (1954).[16] Describing the potential relationship between reader and book, Stevens wrote that "[t]he reader became the book; and summer night [w]as like the conscious being of the book." This blending of reader, summer night, and book was a manifestation of "[t]he truth in a calm world . . . in which there is no other meaning . . ." Stevens' short poem must be read in its entirety. It provides insight into the holistic feeling of flow Marcus described in his *Meditations*.

Gratitude and an orientation toward goodness and beauty

Marcus Aurelius's gratitude statement is also instructive because it suggests that the grateful mind can *visualize* human connection from a distance--both in place and time. Test this idea for yourself. Write a few words of gratitude to a deceased friend or family member. Probably you're seeing this person now. Your memories *bring them alive again*--perhaps the only form of "life after death" we can expect. You may feel some sadness in this context, but the process of expressing gratitude requires a focus on goodness received in the past that can be replicated with others in the present.

Research and experience suggest that the grateful mind is unlikely to be dominated by feelings of emptiness, isolation, hopelessness, anxiety, low self-esteem, and the inability to control a cascade of ugly or negative thoughts and memories. It's likely many religious and philosophical traditions highlight the importance of gratitude[17] for precisely that reason. The Christian tradition, for example, contains this guidance in Philippians 4:8:

> Finally, brothers, whatever is true, whatever is noble, whatever is right, whatever is pure, whatever is lovely, whatever is admirable—if anything is excellent or praiseworthy—think about such things.

Aristotle said much the same:

---

16   Stevens, Wallace, "The House was Quiet and the World was Calm" (1954).

17   See "The Review of Religions" (religious texts on gratitude cited).

> If all people competed for the beautiful, and strained to do the most beautiful things, everything people need in common, and the greatest good for each in particular, would be achieved . . . .[18]

Gratitude and academic success

There's growing evidence that the grateful mind also contributes to academic success. Multiple studies have shown that gratitude enhances motivation,[19] self-control (including resisting the temptation to cheat),[20] and "better learning-related outcomes." [21] All of these favorable results will likely be enhanced if students can be encouraged to develop the habit of keeping a gratitude journal.[22]

Learning is often collegial. Appreciation of goodness received in the past is a likely inducement to cooperative relationships with others in the future. Joel Wong and colleagues found in this regard that "[g]rateful brains . . . seem to place more value on benefits to others" and that "we can see kindness and generously paying it forward as neurologically linked with the experience of gratitude." [23] The grateful brain, in short, will likely be a welcome contributor to any shared endeavor.

---

18   Aristotle, *Nicomachean Ethics* (Sachs, J. trans.; 2002), p. XXIV.

19   Wong, Joel and colleagues, "Why Gratitude is Good for Us" in *The Gratitude Project* (2020), p. 59.

20   Markman, Art, "Gratitude May Increase Self-Control: A New Study Suggests that People who Feel Grateful Resist the Urge to Cheat. *Psychology Today*, October 1, 2019. Markman, a professor of cognitive scientist at the University of Texas, wrote:

> This study suggests that gratitude makes people less likely to cheat. The study didn't explore exactly why gratitude decreases cheating behavior, but this work fits with studies suggesting that gratitude increases people's sense of obligation to others. For example, feeling grateful increases the chances that people will pay debts they owe to others.

21   King, Ronnel and Datu, Jesus Alfonso, "Grateful Students are Motivated, Engaged, and Successful in School: Cross-Sectional, Longitudinal, and Experimental Evidence" *Journal of School Psychology* (2018).

22   Froh, Jeffrey and Bono, Giacomo, "How to Foster Gratitude in Schools" in *The Gratitude Project* (2020), p.160. The authors observed:

> In our research, we've tested concrete ways that educators can actually make youth more grateful—with very positive results. This research points to specific practices and principles that educators can weave into their classrooms. Perhaps the most commonly used technique for boosting gratitude—among adults and youth alike—is a gratitude journal. In one early study, we asked middle-school students simply to list five things for which they were grateful, daily for two weeks, and we compared these students to others who were writing about hassles in their life or basic daily life events. Keeping a gratitude journal was related to more optimism and life satisfaction and to fewer physical complaints and negative emotions. Most significantly, compared to the other students, gratitude journalers reported more satisfaction with their school experience immediately after the two-week period, a result that held up even three weeks later.

23   Wong, Joel and colleagues, "Why Gratitude is Good for Us" in *The Gratitude Project* (2020), p. 56.

Gratitude, human connection, and mental health

A sizable minority of AIS students self-report high levels of anxiety and depression. What AIS tutors see in this regard is consistent with a 2022 *New York Times* feature article documenting an unprecedented "mental health crisis among U.S. teens." [24] The *Times* cited a 2021 report from the U.S. Surgeon General showing dramatic increases in "persistent feelings of sadness or hopelessness;" suicide ideation; psychiatric visits to emergency rooms; and a 57 percent increase in the suicide rate among the 10-24 age group between 2007 and 2018. [25] Comparable data was shared with college administrators in Gary Pavela's May 31, 2019 newsletter article "Beyond Therapy: Providing Guidance to Troubled Students." [26]

Gratitude statements serve as a powerful instrument for both ethical development and therapeutic support. Their dual utility stems from the innate link between gratitude, human connection, and successful adaptation. [27]

Research suggests that gratitude may reduce suicide risk, [28] perhaps by conditioning the grateful mind to seek help from others--including mental health professionals. Professional therapy, in turn, can amplify

---

24   Richtel, Mat, "It's 'Life or Death' The Mental Health Crisis Among U.S. Teens," *New York Times*, April 23, 2022.

25   U.S. Department of Health and Human Services, "Protecting Youth Mental Health: The U.S. Surgeon General's Advisory" (2021)

26   Pavela, Gary, "Beyond therapy: Providing Guidance to Troubled Students," *The Pavela Report*, May 31, 2019.

27   The importance of personal connection (e.g. the therapeutic alliance in talk therapy) is supported by research showing that "[t]he combination of psychotherapy and pharmacotherapy seems to be the best choice for patients with moderate depression." See Cuijpers, Pim, et.al., "A Network Meta-Analysis of the Effects of Psychotherapies, Pharmacotherapies and their Combination in the Treatment of Adult Depression (summary)," *World Psychiatry*, January 10, 2020.

28   Khorrami, Najma, "Can Gratitude Protect Against Suicide?" *Psychology Today*, February 19, 2021. The author wrote:

> In the first adult study looking at gratitude and suicide protection, researchers found that gratitude can buffer against the risk factors of hopelessness and depressive symptoms, which often lead to suicidal ideation and behavior. Kleiman et al. explain that gratitude's ability to produce more positive emotions and more rewarding social interactions are two ways that gratitude protects against suicide. Gratitude's protective role is enabled by generating meaning, belonging, hope, appreciation, and positivity, especially for young adults just beginning to navigate their way in the world.

> A more recent study (in 2020) also supported the hypothesis that gratitude was linked to less suicide risk. This study looked at a gratitude practice among college students. The results also showed that gratitude protects against suicide via benefits to social support and reduced hopelessness.

the power of gratitude by making it habitual, including regular use of gratitude letters and journals.

Indiana University researchers Joshua Brown and Joel Wong have found in this regard that "practicing gratitude" in combination with psychological counseling helps participants shift attention away from "toxic emotions" and has "lasting effects on the brain." They wrote:

> Compared with the participants who wrote about negative experiences or only received counseling, those who wrote gratitude letters reported significantly better mental health four weeks and 12 weeks after their writing exercise ended . . . . In fact, it seems, practicing gratitude on top of receiving psychological counseling carries greater benefits than counseling alone, even when that gratitude practice is brief . . . . Most interestingly, when we compared those who wrote the gratitude letters with those who didn't, the gratitude letter writers showed greater activation in the medial prefrontal cortex when they experienced gratitude in the MRI scanner. This is striking as this effect was found three months after the letter writing began. This indicates that simply expressing gratitude may have lasting effects on the brain.[29]

Gratitude and resilience

We all see a cacophony of social, political, and environmental crises too numerous to list here. How can we invite students to write gratitude statements when there seems so little to be grateful about? The most obvious answer comes from students themselves. They can be lucid about the world around them and still write beautiful gratitude statements thanking friends, family members, teachers, family dogs or cats, and the universe itself. Here's a recent example from an Integrity Seminar student:

> Thanks to the universe. This was all a game of chance, a roll of the die and somehow, I ended up with a lot of good and bad. I received balance and a perspective of my own. I was

---

29 Brown, Joshua, and Wong, Joel, "How Gratitude Changes You and Your Brain," *Greater Good Magazine*, June 6, 2017.

surrounded with people, people who made mistakes but also people who tried and did. To a giant galaxy that I will never comprehend, I say thanks for the good things in my life, the experiences, and the challenges that I have overcome and am facing, the ability to be an artist and the opportunity to be something more than what was expected of me.

Marcus Aurelius wrote his famous gratitude statement in times not unlike our own. He faced revolts, invasions, multiple deaths of friends and family, and the Antonine Plague of 165 to 180 AD--which ultimately caused his death and the death of millions of people throughout the Roman empire. Even in this context, expressing gratitude wasn't a burden. Doing so allowed Marcus to reiterate a fundamental lesson in Stoicism and contemporary cognitive behavioral therapy: *We have at least some control over the focus of our attention.* Shall we dwell among thoughts about a dreadful past or a frightening future, or should we focus on the beauty, goodness, and love we experience now?

Thank you for existing, friends say to one another, and to the world and all the universe. This kind of gratitude is certainly a virtue, for it is the happiness of loving, the only happiness there is. [30]

-- André Comte-Sponville, *A Small Treatise on the Great Virtues*

Understanding this choice helps explain why Stoicism isn't a passive or indifferent philosophy. Without the *awareness of goodness* seen in others and in nature itself, we cannot imagine or strive for *more goodness* in a better world. Marcus uses the word "justice" over a dozen times in his *Meditations* (Gregory Hays translation) [31] and was known for kindness, compassion, and emotional intelligence.

---

30   Comte-Sponville, André, *A Small Treatise on the Great Virtues* (2002), p. 139.

31   Aurelius, Marcus, *Meditations: A New Translation* (Hays, trans., 2003).

Marcus wrote, for example:

> Does what's happened keep you from acting with justice, generosity, self-control, sanity, prudence, honesty, humility, straightforwardness, and all the other qualities that allow a person's nature to fulfill itself? So remember this principle when something threatens to cause you pain: the thing itself was no misfortune at all; to endure it and prevail is great good fortune . . . .[32]
>
> Commitment to justice in your own acts. Which means: thought and action resulting in the common good. What you were born to do.[33]

Human lives are brief and trivial. Yesterday a blob of semen; tomorrow embalming fluid, ash. To pass through this brief life as nature demands. To give it up without complaint. Like an olive that ripens and falls. Praising its mother, thanking the tree it grew on. [34]

---Marcus Aurelius

Marcus transformed a gratitude statement into a Stoic treatise. What relevance can it have now? The Holocaust, for example, is an archetype of evil. How is it even conceivable to imagine a grateful mind dwelling there?

Robert Emmons tells the story of Holocaust survivor Elie Wiesel:

> "Wiesel [transported by cattle car to Auschwitz at age 15] continues to draw on his prison experiences when he explains . . . that people's minds build their prison walls. Their thoughts line them with barbed wire. Internal judgments become the

---

32   Aurelius, Marcus, *Meditations: A New Translation* (Hays, trans.; 2003), pps. 47-48.

33   Aurelius, Marcus, *Meditations: A New Translation* (Hays, trans.; 2003), p. 124.

34   Aurelius, Marcus, *Meditations: A New Translation* (Hays, trans.; 2003), p. 47.

patrolling guards. Escape requires tunneling or climbing through those barriers and walking past the guards.

How does one escape? *For Wiesel, the key that opens the prison door is the key of gratefulness.* Searching for and being thankful for what is positive in every situation digs the tunnel and breaks the stranglehold of despair. Wiesel writes, 'This simple process has the power to transform your life. If the dust settles and you're still standing, there's a reason for it . . . now start walking! You can leave the kingdom of night [35] [emphasis added].

Wiesel elaborated on this theme in his 1986 Nobel Prize speech: [36]

I remember: it happened yesterday or eternities ago. A young Jewish boy discovered the kingdom of night. I remember his bewilderment, I remember his anguish. It all happened so fast. The ghetto. The deportation. The sealed cattle car. The fiery altar upon which the history of our people and the future of mankind were meant to be sacrificed. I remember: he asked his father: "Can this be true?" This is the twentieth century, not the Middle Ages. Who would allow such crimes to be committed? How could the world remain silent? And now the boy is turning to me: "Tell me," he asks. "What have you done with my future? What have you done with your life?"

. . . . This is what I say to the young Jewish boy wondering what I have done with his years. It is in his name that I speak to you and that I express to you my deepest gratitude. *No one is as capable of gratitude as one who has emerged from the kingdom of night. We know that every moment is a moment of grace, every hour an offering; not to share them would mean to betray them. Our lives no longer belong to us alone; they belong to all those who need us desperately* [emphasis added].

---

35   Emmons, Robert, "Thanks: How Practicing Gratitude Can Make you Happier" (2007), pp. 183-184.

36   Wiesel, Elie, Nobel Prize Acceptance Speech (1986).

CHAPTER THREE

KNOW THYSELF
(Self-insight and Self-management)

"Know thyself" > "Nothing to excess" > "Certainty Brings Ruin."
--Three inscriptions from the Temple of Apollo at Delphi [1]

What is the Hokies versus Hoos food fight?

"Hokies" is a nickname for sports fans and teams at Virginia Tech. "Hoos" refers to their counterparts at the University of Virginia. Their "food fight" occurs when they engage in a competitive effort to raise funds for local food banks.

Don't be distracted by the weirdness of team nicknames in Virginia. More important is the effort by VT and UVA alumni associations to transform the tribal energies associated with sport boosterism into a worthy social end. Facebook users, for example, can follow the annual Hokies vs Hoos Food Fight [2] ("a canned food and funds competition between Virginia Tech and UVA") that typically takes place online.

---

1 Pausanias description of Greece at http://bit.ly/3GAN1PG (Perseus Digital Library at Tufts University). The third inscription has multiple interpretations. Classical scholar Eliza Gregory Wilkins wrote in the journal *Classical Philology* (April, 1927) that the ancient Greek historian Diodorus of Sicily favored the view that the maxim *"forbids strong affirmations and emphatically guaranteeing and determining something in human affairs"* (p.126). Wilkins cited another source (Diogenes Laertius) and wrote:

   In view of the setting in which we find the maxim, then, its meaning for Diogenes Laertius becomes clear, and we may construe the passage . . . . "[T]rouble attends him who affirms anything in strong terms and confidently" (p. 129).

   Contemporary usage can be seen at the Econation site.

2 Hokies versus Hoos Facebook page: https://bit.ly/3TvKEng.

Alumni sponsors of the Hokies versus Hoos food fight understood an important concept in neuroscience, psychology, and applied ethics: the capacity for conflict built into the human brain [3] can be used to turn *group rivalry* into *social cooperation.* Doing so entails enhanced partnership between the executive function in the human prefrontal cortex (a part of the brain that encompasses "high-order cognitive abilities" [4]) and the capacity for love and compassion exhibited within "the brain's limbic motivation and reward circuits." [5] We introduce AIS students to this topic (an example of Plato's chariot allegory in action) because we want them to visualize what a skillfully managed brain can accomplish.

Know thyself

"Know thyself" was one of the maxims visible at the entrance to the Temple of Apollo at Delphi. Classical scholar Ingrid Rossellini summarized the meaning:

> The dictum essentially meant this: because the meaning you give to your life is what propels your actions, before asking what to do, ask yourself who you are.[6]

Why explore the topic of self-insight with students in an academic integrity seminar? The answer is that many of them have encountered the consequences of self-defeating behavior and are emotionally and intellectually *ready* to make a change. Author Will Storr described the potential educational impact of such a defining moment:

> Every now and then, actual reality will push back at us. Something in our environment will change in such a way that our flawed models aren't predicting and are, therefore, specifically unable to cope with. We try to contain the chaos but because this change strikes directly against our model's particular flaws, we fail. Then

3   Fields, Douglas, "The Roots of Human Aggression: Experiments in Humans and Animals have Started to Identify how Violent Behaviors Begin in the Brain," *Scientific American*, May 1, 2019.

4   Cristofori, Irene, Cohen-Zimerman, Shira, and Grafman, Jordan Handbook of Clinical Neurology 163 (2019), pp. 197-219.

5   Esch, T, and Stefano, G., "The Neurobiological Link between Compassion and Love," *Medical Science Monitor,* February 25, 2011.

6   Rossellini, Ingrid, *Know Thyself: Western Identity from Classical Greece to the Renaissance* (2018), p. 11.

we can become conflicted. Are we right? Or is there actually a chance we're wrong? If this deep, identity-forming belief turns out to be wrong, then who the hell are we? The dramatic question has been triggered. The story has begun. *Finding out who we are, and who we need to become, means accepting the challenge that story offers us. Are we brave enough to change? This is the question a plot, and a life, asks of each of us* [emphasis added]. [7]

AIS tutors want to reassure students they have multiple ways to reformulate the plot of their lives, all starting with the obligation to "know thyself"--both as an individual and as a member of a fallible, admirable, and deeply conflicted species.

**AN AIS TUTOR COMMENT FREQUENTLY
SHARED WITH STUDENTS:**

The philosopher Nietzsche wrote:
> One can dispose of one's drives like a gardener and, though few know it, cultivate the shoots of anger, pity, [and] vanity, as productively and profitably as a beautiful fruit tree on a trellis.[8]

The key underlying concept is "knowing thyself." With better self-insight, it's possible to determine which of our drives are grounded on short-term desires (like vanity or greed) and how those desires may be cultivated into goals and habits that shape a beautiful life (for example, greed for personal consumption becomes hunger for loving, learning and building).

Trying to understand the maxim "know thyself" begins with an admission of humility. We often seek self-understanding because we've

---

7   Storr, Will, *The Science of Storytelling* (2019), p. 179.

8   Nietzsche, Friedrich, Daybreak, Book V, Aphorism #560 (Nietzsche online reader).

encountered a failure in self-management. Also, from a Greek perspective, individuals cannot reasonably aspire to perfection. At best, we will exhibit only a small spark of the larger "Logos" (the "active rational and spiritual principle that permeate[s] all reality").[9] This kind of *intellectual* humility was evident throughout Greek literature, including a famous observation from Socrates at the end of the *Apology*:

> The hour of departure has arrived, and we go our ways -- I to die, and you to live. *Which is better God only knows* [emphasis added].[10]

In a world and at a time when ultimate questions were decisively answered by revelation and authority, Socrates suggested that the greatest wisdom may be *"I don't know."*[11] His commitment to "creative doubting" --coupled with intellectual curiosity and the capacity for love and friendship[12] --lies at the heart of successful teaching and learning.

---

9   Encyclopedia Britannica, available at https://www.britannica.com/topic/logos.

10   Plato, *Apology* (Jowett, trans.), available at http://classics.mit.edu/Plato/apology.html. See also Comte-Sponville, Andre, *A Small Treatise on the Great Virtues: The Uses of Philosophy in Everyday Life* (2002), p. 140: "Humility is the virtue of the man who knows he is not God."

11   Consider the related insight of poet Wislawa Szymborska in her December 7, 1996 Nobel Prize speech:

> All sorts of torturers, dictators, fanatics, and demagogues struggling for power by way of a few loudly shouted slogans also enjoy their jobs, and they too perform their duties with inventive fervor. Well, yes, but they "know." They know, and whatever they know is enough for them once and for all. They don't want to find out about anything else, since that might diminish their arguments' force. And any knowledge that doesn't lead to new questions quickly dies out: it fails to maintain the temperature required for sustaining life. In the most extreme cases, cases well known from ancient and modern history, it even poses a lethal threat to society.
>
> This is why I value that little phrase "I don't know" so highly. It's small, but it flies on mighty wings. It expands our lives to include the spaces within us as well as those outer expanses in which our tiny Earth hangs suspended. If Isaac Newton had never said to himself "I don't know," the apples in his little orchard might have dropped to the ground like hailstones and at best he would have stooped to pick them up and gobble them with gusto.

12   See Plato's *Gorgias*, Penguin Classics (Hamilton, trans.; 2004 revised edition), p. 107. Socrates' summary:

> This seems to me the goal that one should have in view throughout one's life; we can win happiness only by directing all our own efforts and those of the state to the realization of justice and self-discipline, not by allowing our desires to go unchecked, and, in an attempt to satisfy them, evil without end, leading the life of an outlaw. *A person like this will win the love neither of god nor of his fellow-men; he is incapable of social life, and without social life there can be no friendship.* Wise men say, Callicles, that heaven and earth, gods and men, are held together by *the bonds of community and friendship and order and discipline and righteousness, and that is why the universe, my friend, is called an ordered whole or cosmos and not a state of disorder and license.* You, I think, for all your cleverness, have not paid attention to these matters; you have not observed how great a part geometric equality plays among gods and men, and because you neglect the study of geometry you preach the doctrine of unfair shares (emphasis added).

Expressed as characteristics of emotional intelligence,[13] those qualities are components of human flourishing in multiple dimensions. See our MEDIUM essay "Belief + Doubt = Sanity." [14]

> *One of the most important jobs a teacher has is to allow students to make contact with their ignorance. We need to provide a scene where not-knowing is, at least at the outset, valued more than full, worldly confidence.* [15]
>
> -- Mark Edmundson

A second meaning to "know thyself" is an imperative to know our-selves *as human beings.* What common traits define our shared human nature? Are people *impulsive, selfish, and acquisitive* or *sensible, cooperative and altruistic?* The following observation by Microbiologist René Dubos suggests the answer is *all of the above.*

> Every perceptive adult knows he is part beast and part saint, a mixture of folly and reason, love and hate, courage and cowardice. He can be at the same time believer and doubter, idealist and skeptic, altruistic citizen and selfish hedonist. The coexistence of these conflicting traits naturally causes tension but it is nonetheless compatible with sanity. In a mysterious way, the search for identity and the pursuit of self-selected goals harmonize opposites and facilitate the integration of discordant human traits into some kind of working accord.[16]

---

13   See, generally, Lambert, Craig, "The Emotional Path to Success" in *Harvard Magazine,* September-October 1998.

14   Pavela, Gary, MEDIUM: "Belief + Doubt = Sanity (February 2, 2022).

15   Edmundson, Mark, The Heart of the Humanities: Reading, Writing, Teaching (2018), Kindle location 754 (Part I, "For Ignorance").

16   Dubos, Rene, *A God Within* (1972), p. 84.

The point of life is not to point out the weaknesses of your spouse, your neighbor, or even your political opponent. The point of life is to point out and overcome the weaknesses in ourselves. [17]

--Samuel Wilkinson, Associate Professor of Psychiatry at the Yale School of Medicine

Plato's depiction of the divided brain

An image on a Greek vase appears on our cover. We described it in our introduction and reiterate it here.

Public domain image

---

17   Wilkinson, Samuel, "An Evolutionary Understanding of Our Meaning and Purpose on This Planet," March 22, 2024 *Next Big Idea* magazine (summarizing key points in his March, 2024 book *Purpose: What Evolution and Human Nature Imply about the Meaning of Our Existence*). See a related review of Wilkinson's book by philosopher John Kaag in the March 4, 2024 American Scholar ("The Choice Is Ours"): Kaag wrote:

In *Purpose* . . . [Wilkinson] bids that readers consider what might be called an argument from experience: *What are some of the most meaningful moments of your life?* For most of us, our answers are borne out by research. Psychologists have found that people tend to find sustained loving relationships to be among the most meaningful aspects of life . . . .

Wilkinson's description of our nature deserves a hearing: In order to inspire and protect meaningful relationships, human beings have to negotiate their 'dual potentials' carefully. We don't have to be perfect, but we do, on balance, have to make the right decisions day after day, year after year. Every world religion, every great spiritual or wisdom tradition, has this idea stitched into its moral fabric (emphasis added].

In his dialogue *Phaedrus*, Plato wrote:

> *Of the nature of the soul let me speak briefly, and in a figure. And let the figure be composite -- a pair of winged horses and a charioteer. Now the winged horses and the charioteers of the gods are all of them noble . . . but those of other beings are mixed; the human charioteer drives his in a pair; and one of them is noble and the other is ignoble; and the driving of them of necessity gives a great deal of trouble to him.*[18]

Whatever the original creator of the pictured vase intended, we will refer to it here as "Plato's Chariot." To us, the horses represent two parts of the human *limbic system* ("the center of advanced emotionality"),[19] while the driver might be equated to the *executive function*. The reins are also important. They can be understood as *reciprocal messaging pathways* between the executive function and other parts of the brain, including the limbic system. Those pathways develop on their own schedule and play an important role in impulse control.[20]

It's tempting to see the "ignoble" horse as a harmful vestige of a primitive mind. This ancient component, however, may be essential to human flourishing. Beyond the added power of two horses rather than one (two draft horses working together can pull about three times as much as one horse [21]), horses with differing temperaments add an element of creative energy chariot drivers may welcome.

---

18   Plato, *Phaedrus* (Jowett, trans., 2012) p. 14.

19   Lewis, Thomas, Amini, Fari, and Lannon, Richard, A General Theory of Love (2001), p. 58.

20   Daniel J. Siegel (clinical professor of psychiatry at the UCLA School of Medicine) explored this topic in his book: Brainstorm: The Power and Purpose of the Teenage Brain (2014). He wrote:

> . . . impulses can be put on hold if certain fibers in the higher part of the brain work to create a mental space between impulse and action. It is during the time of adolescence that these regulatory fibers begin to grow to counteract the revved-up "go" of the dopamine reward system. The result is a decrease in impulsivity. This is sometimes called "cognitive control" and is one important source of diminished danger and reduced risks as adolescents develop (p. 68).

21   See Grisham, Molly, "The Strength of Teams" Influence LLC. Website (undated).

Individual selection favors what we call sin and group selection favors virtue.... The instability of the emotions is a quality we should wish to keep. It is the essence of the human character, and the source of our creativity.... We must learn to behave, but let us never even think of domesticating human nature. [22]

--E.O. Wilson (University Research Professor Emeritus at Harvard and a winner of the National Medal of Science)

A divided brain and a functioning whole

Constituent parts of the body communicate with the brain in ways that enhance our capacity for sympathy and cooperation.[23] The end result can help explain consciousness itself. [24] Much like Plato's chariot--which has multiple components that serve a common function--the brain must be seen both as divided *and* as a functioning whole. This is a remarkably intricate structure, complicated by the fact that "emotions reach back 100 million years, while cognition is a few hundred thousand years old

---

22   Wilson, E. O. The Meaning of Human Existence (2014), p. 179-180.

23   Keltner, Dacher *Born to Be Good: The Science of a Meaningful Life* (2009), p. 228:

> In calling sympathy the strongest of instincts, Darwin was touching a nerve in the veins of canonical Western thought. Little did he know, Darwin was also touching another nerve, literally a bundle of nerves, known as the vagus nerve, which resides in the chest and, when activated, produces a feeling of spreading, liquid warmth in the chest and a lump in the throat. The vagus nerve originates in the top of the spinal cord and then winds its way through the body (vagus is Latin for wandering), connecting up to facial muscle tissue, muscles that are involved in vocalization, the heart, the lungs, the kidneys and liver, and the digestive organs. In a series of controversial papers, physiological psychologist Steve Porges has made the case that the vagus nerve is the nerve of compassion, the body's caretaking organ.

24   See Damasio, Antonio, "Being, Feeling, and Knowing: Our Path to Consciousness," *New Scientist,* November 1, 2021:

> It is likely true that consciousness only emerges in organisms endowed with nervous systems, but it is just as true that consciousness also requires abundant interactions between those systems and many non-nervous parts of the organism . . . . What the rest of the body brings to the marriage with the nervous system is billions of years of complex biological intelligence, the covert competence that sustains life by satisfying the demands of life regulation and maintaining homeostasis. What nervous systems bring to the marriage is the possibility of making biological intelligence *explicit,* by constructing the patterns of neural activation that constitute neural maps and mental images. The result of this process is explicit knowledge of the body and the world around it.

at best." [25] The limbic horses, in short, likely pose an even greater challenge to the chariot driver than Plato imagined.

Antonio Damasio (Chair in Neuroscience, as well as Professor of Psychology, Philosophy, and Neurology, at the University of Southern California) wrote:

> The nervous system, including its natural core, the brain, is located in its entirety within the territory of the body proper and is fully conversant with it. As a consequence, body and nervous system can interact directly and abundantly . . . . An astonishing consequence of this peculiar arrangement is that feelings are not conventional perceptions of the body but rather hybrids, at home in both body and brain. This hybrid condition may help explain why there is a profound distinction but no opposition between feeling and reason, why we are feeling creatures that think and thinking creatures that feel. We go through life feeling or reasoning or both, as required by the circumstances. Human nature benefits from an abundance of explicit and non-explicit types of intelligence and from the use of feeling and reason, each alone or in combination.[26]

Philosopher Martha Nussbaum said much the same:

> Instead of viewing morality as a system of principles to be grasped by the detached intellect, and emotions as motivations that either support or subvert our choice to act according to principle, we will have to consider emotions as part and parcel of the system of ethical reasoning. We cannot plausibly omit them, once we acknowledge that emotions include in their content judgments that can be true or false, and good or bad guides to ethical choice.[27]

How might emotion and reason *blend* as "part and parcel" of ethical decision making? Nussbaum wrote that "[i]nternal to our emotional response itself is the judgment that what is at issue is indeed

25 Lewis, Thomas, Amini, Fari, and Lannon, Richard, *A General Theory of Love* (2001), p. 240.

26 Damasio, Antonio, *Feeling and Knowing: Making Minds Conscious* (2021), p. 6.

27 Nussbaum, Martha, *Upheavals of Thought: The Intelligence of Emotions* (2003), p. 1.

serious–has *'size,'* as Aristotle puts it . . . . "Losing a toothbrush, for example "does not occasion even a mild grief" and "someone who takes a paperclip off my desk does not make me even a tiny bit angry."[28] Feelings, in other words, can contain rational components reflecting the severity of a loss.

Nussbaum is not contending that feelings are inherently self-regulating. A child, for example, could foreseeably experience an emotional "meltdown" due to the loss of an item regarded as trivial by an adult. That possibility suggests that the mature "judgment" Nussbaum has in mind encompasses ethical decision-making shaped by *example, experience, training, and habituation*[29] Aristotle made the same point in one of his most cited passages:

> [S]o, too, any one can get angry—that is easy—or give or spend money; but to do this to the right person, to the right extent, at the right time, with the right motive, and in the right way, that is not for everyone, nor is it easy; wherefore goodness is both rare and laudable and noble . . . . [30]

Aristotle did not disparage emotions, including anger. He believed they can be "laudable and noble" if properly managed. Basically, Aristotle was highlighting qualities that Plato (his teacher) would have seen as complementary attributes of the "noble" and "ignoble" horses pulling his allegorical chariot.

It's challenging to identify any precise point in the brain where emotions and cognition interact. Perhaps the intersection occurs in what is known as the insular or "limbic integration" cortex,[31] or throughout

---

28   Nussbaum, Martha, *Upheavals of Thought: The Intelligence of Emotions* (2003), p. 1.

29   Aristotle, Nicomachean Ethics, (Ross, trans., republished 2016), p. 27.

> For the things we have to learn before we can do them, we learn by doing them, e.g. men become builders by building and lyreplayers by playing the lyre; so too we become just by doing just acts, temperate by doing temperate acts, brave by doing brave acts . . . . It makes no small difference, then, whether we form habits of one kind or of another from our very youth; it makes a very great difference, or rather all the difference.

30   Aristotle, Nicomachean Ethics, (Ross, trans., republished 2016), pp 36-37.

31   Uddin L. Q., Nomi J. S., Hébert-Seropian B., Ghaziri J., and Boucher, O. Structure and Function of the Human Insula. *J Clin Neurophysiol.* (2017), 34(4), pp. 300-306.

the body. [32] Whatever the source, one of the most important outcomes of the intersection is *conscience.* No one better described the origins of conscience than Charles Darwin:

> A moral being is one who is capable of reflecting on his past actions and their motives—of approving of some and disapproving of others; and the fact that man is the one being who certainly deserves this designation, is the greatest of all distinctions between him and the lower animals . . . . Owing to this condition of mind, man cannot avoid looking both backwards and forwards, and comparing past impressions. Hence after some temporary desire or passion has mastered his social instincts, he reflects and compares the now weakened impression of such past impulses with the ever-present social instincts; and he then feels that sense of dissatisfaction which all unsatisfied instincts leave behind them, he therefore resolves to act differently for the future,—*and this is conscience . . . .*

> The moral nature of man has reached its present standard, partly through the advancement of his reasoning powers and consequently of a just public opinion, *but especially from his sympathies having been rendered more tender and widely diffused through the effects of habit, example, instruction, and reflection . . .* [emphasis added]. [33]

Darwin highlighted the importance of conscience outside a traditional religious context. Doing so made his views credible to Sigmund Freud, who saw similar qualities in his concept of a *superego.*[34] However defined, the origins and role of conscience need more attention in pertinent conversations with students. Amit Sood (past director of research in the Complementary and Integrative Medicine Program at

---

32   Keltner, Dacher *Born to Be Good: The Science of a Meaningful Life* (2009), p. 228.

33   Darwin, Charles, *Descent of Man,* Chapter XXI (1874, second edition, published in "Darwin, Norton Critical Edition," 1979), pp. 200-201.

34   *Encyclopedia Britannica* entry, "Conscience:" The entry states:

> Another explanation of conscience was put forth in the 20th century by Sigmund Freud in his postulation of the superego. According to Freud, the superego is a major element of personality that is formed by the child's incorporation of moral values through parental approval or punishment. The resulting internalized set of prohibitions, condemnations, and inhibitions is that part of the superego known as conscience.

the Mayo Clinic) provided an evocative description of how conscience can speak to each of us:

> Although conscience always has an opinion, it speaks in a humble, low volume, easily drowned by the vortices of the mind and the senses.[35]

Helping students hear the voice of conscience starts by acknowledging its existence. The Academic Integrity Seminar does so in several assignments, including the Gratitude Statement, a Confucian allegory by the ancient philosopher Mengzi, and an interview with psychiatrist Roberto Assagioli.[36]

The technique of inner dialogue works well. Imagine a very wise person who knows the answers to all the problems you face. If you could obtain an interview with this person what would she tell you? This is your inner teacher....[37]

-- Roberto Assagioli, MD

Many books have and will be devoted to the topic of discordant components of the human mind. A compelling example of the complementary and competing aspects of reason and emotion was stated in a recollection by Thomas Jefferson about his teachers at the College of William and Mary.[38]

> Under temptations and difficulties I could ask myself what would Dr. Small, Mr. Wythe, Peyton Randolph do in this situation? What course in it will assure me of their approbation? *I am*

---

35   Sood, Amit, "Something to Think About: Listen to the Conscience," Mayo Clinic News Network, July 7, 2016.

36   Our current AIS assignments can be seen at this link: https://bit.ly/3YUMW0Z.

37   Assagioli, Roberto. Interview with Sam Keen in "The Golden Mean of Roberto Assagioli," *Psychology Today,* December 1974 (reprinted at the Kenneth Sorenson psychosynthesis website).

38   Letter from Thomas Jefferson to Thomas Jefferson Randolph, 24 November 1808.

certain that this mode of deciding on my conduct tended more to its correctness than any reasoning power I possessed [emphasis added].

In this key passage Jefferson employed *reason* to emphasize the importance of *limbic connections* between teacher and student.

When the limbic brain goes astray

Emotions associated with the limbic system--like the divergent horses on the vase-- can bring out the worst or best in us. Three prominent psychiatrists explored this topic in their book *A General Theory of Love*:

> The evolution of the limbic brain a hundred million years ago created animals with luminescent powers of emotionality and relatedness, their nervous systems designed to intertwine and support each other like supple strands of a vine. But in life, as on the Greek stage, every attribute confers a matching vulnerability; each heroic strength finds its mirror image in a tragic flaw. So it is with the neural skills that constitute emotional life. The limbic brain bestows experiential riches denied simpler creatures, but it also opens mammals up to torment and destruction.[39]

An example of "torment and destruction" caused by the limbic brain in a higher education setting can be found in "A description of student life at the University of Paris" by thirteenth-century churchman Jacques de Vitry:

> Very few [students] studied for their own edification, or that of others. They wrangled and disputed not merely about the various sects or about some discussions; but the differences between the countries also caused dissensions, hatreds and virulent animosities among them and they impudently uttered all kinds of affronts and insults against one another. They affirmed that the English were drunkards and had tails; the sons of France proud, effeminate and carefully adorned like women. They said that the Germans were furious and obscene at their feasts; the Normans, vain and boastful; the Potevins, traitors and always

---

39   Lewis, Thomas, Amini, Fari, and Lannon, Richard, *A General Theory of Love* (2001), p. 204.

adventurers. The Burgundians they considered vulgar and stupid. The Bretons were reputed to be fickle and changeable, and were often reproached for the death of Arthur. The Lombards were called avaricious, vicious and cowardly; the Romans, seditious, turbulent and slanderous; the Sicilians, tyrannical and cruel, the inhabitants of Brabent, men of blood, incendiaries, brigands and ravishers; the Flemish, fickle, prodigal, gluttonous, yielding as butter, and slothful. After such insults from words they often came to blows.[40]

Jacques de Vitry's historical account shows how one part of the limbic brain fulfills a function grounded in distrust of other groups.[41] This function arose and persists because it sometimes serves an evolutionary purpose.[42] The management of our emotions frequently goes astray--in the words of Daniel Goleman--because "we too often

---

40   Fordham University: Medieval Sourcebook: Jacques de Vitry: Life of the Students at Paris.

41   One of the best summaries on this topic can be found in E. O. Wilson's *Social Conquest of the Earth* (2012). Wilson was Pellegrino University Research Professor Emeritus at Harvard University, a Member of the National Academy of Sciences, a winner of the National Medal of Science, and a recipient of two Pulitzer Prizes for General Nonfiction. He wrote:

> The expected consequences of this evolutionary process in humans are the following: • Intense competition occurs between groups, in many circumstances including territorial aggression. • Group composition is unstable, because of the advantage of increasing group size accruing from immigration, ideological proselytization, and conquest, pitted against the opportunities to gain advantage by usurpation within the group and fission to create new groups. • An unavoidable and perpetual war exists between honor, virtue, and duty, the products of group selection, on one side, and selfishness, cowardice, and hypocrisy, the products of individual selection, on the other side. • The perfecting of quick and expert reading of intention in others has been paramount in the evolution of human social behavior. • Much of culture, including especially the content of the creative arts, has arisen from the inevitable clash of individual selection and group selection. In summary, the human condition is an endemic turmoil rooted in the evolution processes that created us. The worst in our nature coexists with the best, and so it will ever be. To scrub it out, if such were possible, would make us less than human (p.56).

42   See, generally, Fields, Douglas, "The Roots of Human Aggression: Experiments in humans and animals have started to identify how violent behaviors begin in the brain," *Scientific American*, May 1, 2019. Fields reported:

> Physical, sometimes deadly violence is the hub of nature's survival-of-the-fittest struggle, and all animals have evolved specialized neural circuitry to execute—and control—aggressive behavior. In pioneering experiments on cats beginning in the late 1920s, Walter Hess discovered a locus deep within the hypothalamus, a brain area that unleashes violent aggression. It turns out that this is the same spot where other powerful compulsive urges and behaviors are activated, including sex, eating and drinking. When Hess stimulated this knot of neurons using a wire electrode inserted into the brain of a docile cat, the feline instantly launched into a hissing rage, attacking and killing another animal in its cage. The human brain has this same neural structure, labeled the hypothalamic attack area.

confront postmodern dilemmas with an emotional repertoire tailored to the urgencies of the Pleistocene." [43]

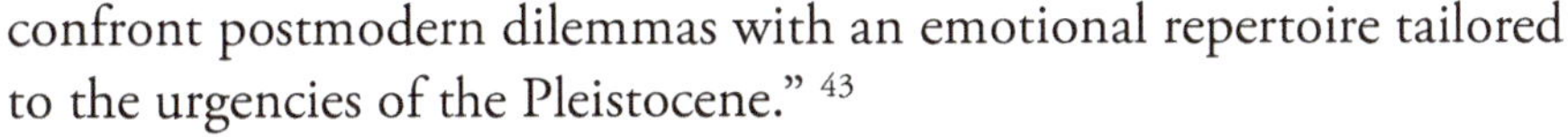

Out of the crooked timber of humanity, no straight thing was ever made. [44]

--Immanuel Kant

Frederick Douglass saw this characteristic from a broader perspective in a magnificent speech ("The Composite Nation") assigned to AIS students:

> To the Hindu, every man not twice born, is Mleeka. To the Greek, every man not speaking Greek, is a barbarian. To the Jew, every one not circumcised, is a gentile. To the Mahometan, every man not believing in the prophet, is a kaffe. I need not repeat here the multitude of reproachful epithets expressive of the same sentiment among ourselves. All who are not to the manor born, have been made to feel the lash and sting of these reproachful names. [45]

The "ignoble horse" of pseudo-Darwinism

Impulsive, selfish, and acquisitive aspects of the human brain can be seen in multiple forms of misconduct, including academic dishonesty. [46] For example, a sizeable minority of AIS students express opinions similar to what a candid high school student said in a CNN interview:

> What's important is getting ahead . . . . The better grades you have, the better school you get into, the better you're going to do in life. And if you learn to cut corners to do that, you're

---

43   Goleman, Daniel, *Emotional Intelligence: Why It Can Matter More Than IQ* (2005), p. 5.

44   Kant, Immanuel, *Idea for a Universal History with a Cosmopolitan Purpose* ("Crooked Timber" source identified). See: "The Crooked Timber of Humanity: Chapters in the History of Ideas, by Isaiah Berlin – Review" in the July 23, 2013 issue of the *Guardian*.

45   Douglass, Frederick, "A Composite Nation" (1867) in the online archive "Black Past."

46   Portions of this section previously appeared in Gary Pavela's *Law and Policy Report* newsletter.

going to be saving yourself time and energy. In the real world, that's what's going to be going on. The better you do, that's what shows. It's not how moral you were in getting there.[47]

This perspective was also concisely stated in an AIS student answer: *"I think that in a dog-eat-dog world people need to be more aggressive to get what they want."*

Forming a definitive world view at age 18 (or any other time) is perilous. It's especially troubling when young people confidently express what might be called "pseudo-Darwinism"-- perhaps because they mistakenly assume it has a scientific foundation. The most extreme example of this phenomenon can be seen in the 2001 Columbine Commission Report, which stated that the Columbine shooters (Eric Harris and Dylan Klebold) believed:

> [T]hey had evolved above "you humans." The two seemed fascinated with the notion of natural selection: "whatever happened to natural selection?" Klebold asked on the tapes as he spoke of his hatred of the human race. On his web page Harris called natural selection ". . . the best thing that has ever happened to the Earth. Getting rid of all the stupid and weak organisms. . . ." Harris also inscribed in a female friend's 1998 yearbook that "natural selection needs a boost, like me with a shotgun." At the time of his death, Harris was wearing a T-shirt with the words "Natural Selection" printed across the front.[48]

Challenging "pseudo-Darwinism" is one of the aims of the Academic Integrity Seminar. We do so by teaching insights that reiterate the partnership between Plato's driver and both limbic horses *working in tandem.* This approach encourages students to combine reason *and* emotion in ways likely to create a foundation of trust for themselves and others.[49]

---

47   CNN, "Many High School Students Don't Think There's Anything Wrong With Cheating," April 5, 2002.

48   Report of the Colorado Columbine Review Commission (2001), p.22, footnote 51.

49   See Brooks, Arthur, "How Smart People Can Stop Being Miserable," *The Atlantic*, March 23, 2023. Brooks wrote:

> [T]he idea that if one person has more, someone else must have less is almost always wrong. A sophisticated understanding of human relationships—which, I should note, requires intelligence—reveals that we interact in a positive-sum world when we work together and assist one

Evoking the better angels of human nature: empathy and reciprocity

Students who describe living in a *dog-eat-dog world* have seen a partial reality. We don't challenge that perception, but urge them to expand their horizons. What's missing is an insight expressed by New York University research professor Ralph Gomory (a recipient of the National Medal of Science):

> Evolution has produced *two sides* of human nature: the more self-centered *and the more altruistic.* Different training and circumstances can bring out in us more of one or the other, but they are both in our DNA [emphasis added].[50]

Perhaps the best refutation of pseudo-Darwinism comes from Darwin himself (see the extended selection from his *Descent of Man* in the section *"A divided brain and a functioning whole"*). Basically, Darwin highlighted the human capacity for *empathy* and *reciprocity,* not domination and exploitation. Selfish and aggressive instincts may be part of our nature, but those instincts can be overcome by empathy, conscience, reason, habituation, and examples of admirable behavior we see in others.

Where might the development of empathy and reciprocity lead? Darwin saw the direction--guided by reason and habit--as leading to "the golden rule" (reciprocity).

> The moral sense perhaps affords the best and highest distinction between man and the lower animals; but I need not say anything on this head, as I have so lately endeavoured to shew that the social instincts,—the prime principle of man's moral constitution—with the aid of active intellectual powers and the effects of habit, naturally lead to the golden rule . . . . and this lies at the foundation of morality [Darwin's related footnote No. 39 cites: "The Thoughts of Marcus Aurelius, etc., p. 139"]. [51]

---

another. Perhaps you believe that helping others succeed economically raises overall prosperity, including your own. If so, using your intellect to lift up others should be, well, a no-brainer.

50　Gomory, Ralph, "Put human nature back in business," *Washington Post,* June 28, 2013.

51　Darwin, Charles, *Descent of Man,* (1871 edition), p. 106.

This passage is one of five instances in his *Essential Works* when Darwin cited the views of Marcus Aurelius. We share it with students and remind them about the gratitude statement they completed early in the Seminar. Both they and Marcus expressed gratitude to people who displayed social and moral qualities Darwin identified as "the best and highest distinction between man and the lower animals."

**AN AIS TUTOR COMMENT FREQUENTLY
SHARED WITH STUDENTS:**

Charles Darwin and the Golden Rule

Charles Darwin emphasized the importance of The Golden Rule in The Descent of Man. *You can also see the rule referenced in many of the world's great religious and philosophical traditions.[52] In China it was stated by Confucius in Analects XV. In the Hindu tradition it can be seen in the Mahabharata (3000 BC); in Islam it can be found in An-Nawawi's Forty Hadith 13); in Judaism you will find it in Talmud Shabbat 31a. In Christianity it is found in Matthew 7:12. An idea all these diverse traditions converge upon is likely to have merit.*

The Golden Rule doesn't fit all circumstances. Individuals who might be defined as psychopaths or masochists, for example, would likely apply the rule in ways Darwin didn't have in mind. Fortunately, most people don't fall into those categories. For them, the Golden Rule is an actionable ethical starting point for using conscience and what Darwin called our "active intellectual powers" to better understand and empathize with others.

---

52   "Living Peace International" website, The Golden Rule (2016).

Why would Darwin emphasize reciprocity as a foundation for human ethical development? Research by Rodolfo Cortes Barragan and Carol S. Dweck at Stanford University suggests reciprocity can become a "critical cue" for higher levels of altruism:

> We began our investigation by examining whether a simple experience with reciprocity might serve as a critical cue for altruism. We found support for this contention. Reciprocal interactions triggered high levels of altruistic behavior on the part of 1-and 2-year olds whereas parallel play did not. Moreover, we found this with an age group in which altruism had been depicted as occurring naturally and without much need for social input. We further found that an even short-er reciprocal interaction elicited substantially more altruism than a parallel interaction in preschoolers and that these in-teractions yielded not only the enactment of altruism but the expectation of it from others. Thus, consistent with anthropo-logical, economic, evolutionary, philosophical, psychological, and sociological theories of human contractual processes, our young participants were, in a sense, capable of drawing broad inferences about the benevolent norm of the situation on *the basis of reciprocal patterns of behavior* [emphasis added].[53]

A Confucian perspective--with new scientific foundations--on goodness and beauty in human nature

A school of Confucion thought associated with the philosopher Mengzi [54] goes beyond reciprocity to emphasize beauty, benevolence, and righteousness in human nature. Mengzi wrote:

> That which people are capable of without learning is their gen-uine capability. That which they know without pondering is their genuine knowledge. Among babes in arms there are none that do not know to love their parents. When they grow older, there are none that do not know to revere their elder brothers.

---

53   Barragan, Rodolfo Cortes and Dweck, Carol, "Rethinking Natural Altruism: Simple Reciprocal Interactions Trigger Children's Benevolence, *Psychological and Cognitive Sciences* (November 17, 2014).

54   See Mencius (Mengzi) in the Stanford Encyclopedia of Philosophy.

Treating one's parents as parents is benevolence. Revering one's elders is righteousness. There is nothing else to do but extend these to the world.[55]

We introduce AIS students to this perspective as an end in itself, but also to emphasize recent scientific insights broadly supporting Mengzi's view that what people "know without pondering" is their "genuine [moral] knowledge."

By reason could I have arrived at knowing that I must love my neighbor and not oppress him? I was told that in childhood, and I believed it gladly, for they told me what was already in my soul. But who discovered it? Not reason. Reason discovered the struggle for existence, and the law that requires us to oppress all who hinder the satisfaction of our desires. That is the deduction of reason. But loving one's neighbor, reason could never discover, because it's unreasonable. [56]

--Leo Tolstoy, *Anna Karenina*

---

55   Cited in Schwitzgebel, Eric "How Mengzi Came up with Something Better than the Golden Rule" *Aeon*, November 1, 2019.

56   Tolstoy, Leo, *Anna Karenina*, Part 8, Chapter Twelve (1877). Leo Tolstoy Archive at http://bit.ly/3Js5fFR

AIS SAMPLE EXERCISE

Please read the following passage from "The Trees of the Niu Mountain" by Mengzi.[57]

The trees of the Niu mountain were once beautiful. Being situated, however, in the borders of a large State, they were cut down with axes . . . . Could they still retain their beauty? And yet, through the regenerative powers of the vegetative life, day and night, and the nourishing influence of the rain and dew, the plants were not without buds and sprouts springing forth. But then came cattle and goats, and browsed upon them. To these things is owing the bare and stripped appearance of the mountain which, when people see it, they think it was never finely wooded. But is what they see the nature of the mountain?

And so also of what properly belongs to man: shall it be said that the mind of any man was without benevolence and righteousness? The way in which a man loses his proper goodness of mind is like the way in which the trees are denuded by axes . . . . Cut down day after day, can the mind retain its beauty? But there is a development of its life day and night, and in the calm air of the morning, just between night and day, the mind feels in a degree those desires and aversions which are proper to humanity; but the feeling is not strong, and it is shackled and destroyed by what takes place during the day. This destruction taking place again and again, the restorative influence of the night is not sufficient to preserve the proper goodness of the mind. And when this proves insufficient for that

---

57   AIS exercise on "The Trees of Niu Mountain" by Mengzi from humanistictexts.org.

purpose, man's nature becomes not much different from that of the irrational animals. When they see this, people think that the mind never had those powers which I assert. But does this condition represent the feelings proper to humanity?

Therefore, if it receives its proper nourishment, there is nothing which will not grow. If it loses its proper nourishment, there is nothing which will not decay away.

Question for you to answer:

Mengzi also wrote: "Persons who have developed their hearts and minds to the utmost know their true nature."

How does Mengzi define our "true [human] nature?" Please cite specific language from "The Trees of Niu Mountain" to support your position.

I liked the Mengzi and Assagioli readings because they focused on redemption and rehabilitation. It is nice to have the reassurance that despite past mistakes I can grow and learn from them. I am not an inherently bad person, I just need to work harder to strengthen my character. Moving forward I am going to be more intentional and reflective of my actions and work to create a positive mindset and habits. This seminar has shown me the importance of ethical and responsible behavior and I will adjust my priorities accordingly.

-- AIS student comment

Students quickly see that Mengzi identifies "proper goodness of mind" (benevolence and righteousness) as core components of human nature. Those components--like nature itself--can be "cut down," but may recover their beauty if "restorative influences" are sufficient to the task. Anyone feeling shame or regret for academic misconduct would likely welcome that perspective.

> *The assignment about Mengzi's writing also reassured me how I can recover from wrongdoings with the right state of mind and proper nourishment, which was a nice reminder that I can still right my wrongs by doing the right action in my future.*
>
> -- AIS student comment

Mengzi famously identified feelings of "compassion, shame, respect, and the ability to approve or disapprove" as inherent capacities in human nature that could be "cultivated" into "corresponding virtues." [58] It's fascinating to see how that ancient perspective echoes the work of Charles Darwin and contemporary research on the human moral sense.

Can the moral capacity Mengzi identified be trained and habitualized? The answer is *yes*, as suggested by Robert Sapolsky, Professor, Neurology and Neurological Sciences at Stanford University. Sapolsky cited research showing that cheaters, for example, won't cheat at "every opportunity" because they frequently engage in "major neurobiological Sturm und Drang" beforehand.[59] What educators should strive for in this regard is what Sapolsky calls *"automaticity"* --quickly and habitually tapping into the limbic capacity for cooperation and good character identified by Mengzi and fostered by disciplined management of Plato's chariot. The process of resisting contrary temptations, Sapolsky wrote, should be made as implicit as:

---

58   Ramsey, John, Mengzi's Moral Psychology, Part 1: The Four Moral Sprouts, April 10, 2018.

59   Sapolsky, Robert, Behave: The Biology of Humans at Our Best and Worst (2017), p. 519.

> Thinking 'Wednesday' after hearing 'Monday, Tuesday,' or as that first piece of regulation we mastered way back when, being potty trained . . . . [I]t's not a function of what Kohlbergian stage you're at; it's what moral imperatives have been hammered into you with such urgency and consistency that doing the right thing has virtually become a spinal reflex . . . .
>
> We've seen something equivalent with the brave act, the person who, amid the paralyzed crowd, runs into the burning building to save the child. "What were you thinking when you decided to go into the house?" (Were you thinking about the evolution of cooperation, of reciprocal altruism, of game theory and reputation?) *And the answer is always "I wasn't thinking anything. Before I knew it, I had run in."* Interviews of Carnegie Medal recipients about that moment shows precisely that—a first, intuitive thought of needing to help, resulting in the risking of life without a second thought. *"Heroism feels and never reasons,"* to quote Emerson [emphasis added].[60]

As we have suggested in other contexts, one of the aims behind academic honor codes is to employ role modeling, appeals to conscience and community, timely reminders (e.g., honor pledges), and the slow accreditation of tradition to evoke a sensibility (in Sapolsky's words) that "doing the right thing . . . virtually become[s] a spinal reflex." One relevant strategy pioneered by schools with traditional or modified honor codes [61] is fostering *intentional* ethical role modeling in campus programs. Consider, for example, the Stanford "What Matters to Me and Why" forums, designed to "encourage reflection within the Stanford Community on matters of personal values, beliefs, and motivations in order to better understand the lives and inspirations of those who shape the University." [62] Intellectual content in the forums

---

60   Sapolsky, Robert, Behave: The Biology of Humans at Our Best and Worst (2017), pp. 519-520.

61   See McCabe, Don, and Pavela, Gary, "New Honor Codes for a New Generation" *Inside Higher Education*, March 11, 2005.

62   Stanford University "What Matters to Me and Why Forums." The site contains this opening statement:

> The purpose of What Matters to Me and Why is to encourage reflection within the Stanford community on matters of personal values, beliefs, and motivations in order to better understand the lives and inspirations of those who shape the University. The presenter is encouraged

is often memorable. Equally impactful is the subliminal message that personal values, beliefs, and motivations are exemplified by speakers who lead lives of integrity. Public sponsorship by a student Honor Council further enhances that impact by fostering supportive peer influence in multiple campus settings.

> *I believe there exists, & I feel within me, an instinct for truth, or knowledge or discovery, of something same nature as the instinct of virtue, & that our having such an instinct is reason enough for scientific researches without any practical results ever ensuing from them.*[63]
>
> --Charles Darwin

An example of Sapolsky's conclusion about the importance of "automaticity" appeared in the national media as this chapter was being written. In an article titled "When Little Leaguers Set the Example for Adults," the *Journal* reported that "Kaiden 'Bubs' Shelton threw a pitch that veered dangerously inside and *thunnnnnk*—it smacked right off the protective helmet of Tulsa batter Isaiah 'Zay' Jarvis, who dropped to the ground and clutched his head." In a video and photo transmitted around the world, Jarvis walked to the pitcher's mound and "embraced his opponent, reassuring him that he was OK." *Jarvis later said "it wasn't really a thought. It was just kind of like a natural reaction"* [emphasis added].[64]

We shared a different example of Sapolsky's "automaticity" in Chapter One (The Power of Stories). A courageous graduate student reported a research mistake that required retraction of a journal article and wrote:

---

to share how s/he has chosen to live her/his life, the core values s/he has adopted, and the personal choices s/he has made. We also encourage the presenter to choose any other topic that fits her/his definition of "what matters to me and why."

63   Darwin, Charles, Letter to John Stevens Henslow (April 1, 1848) Cambridge University Darwin Correspondence Project.

64   Gay, Jason, When Little Leaguers Set the Example for Adults, *Wall Street Journal*, August 15, 2022.

When I discovered the contamination, I could have quietly moved on and likely nobody would have ever known. Some selfish, anxious part of me wanted to do that. But I believe in the importance of intellectual honesty and owning my mistakes and *never seriously flirted with the idea of burying them . . . . [emphasis added].*[65]

[R]eason is, and ought only to be the slave of the passions, and can never pretend to any other office than to serve and obey them.[66]

--David Hume

"Automaticity" can also be driven by short-term thinking and selfishness (unmanaged qualities of Plato's "ignoble" horse). Psychologist Jonathan Haidt's preferred metaphor in this regard is of an elephant and a rider. The elephant represents powerful impulses the rider typically seeks to justify rather than control. Still, at multiple locations in his book *The Righteous Mind,* Haidt indicates that elephants may sometimes see riders as "useful advisor[s]" [67] and be open to rider "persuasion." [68] Those observations suggest that Haidt's metaphorical elephant--like the limbic brain itself-- may be struggling with contending perspectives and alternative responses. The courageous graduate student cited above, for example, wrote about *"some selfish, anxious part of me"* in tension with an equally fast and more compelling *feeling* of integrity. Plato's image of "noble" and "ignoble" horses better captures these kinds of inner conflicts. Reason may have subsequent explanatory power, but *every part* of Plato's chariot--including the driver-- appears to have limbic components seeking to establish and maintain an admirable balance.

---

65   Strassmann, Joan E. (research team lead professor), "Retraction with Honor" (Blog).

66   Hume, David, "A Treatise of Human Nature" (originally published in 1739) Book 3, Part 3, p. 3.

67   Haidt, Jonathan, *The Righteous Mind: Why Good People Are Divided by Politics and Religion* (2013), p. 66.

68   Haidt, Jonathan, *The Righteous Mind: Why Good People Are Divided by Politics and Religion* (2013), p. 64.

The world "admirable" in the last sentence was deliberate. It suggests that ethics and aesthetics should be combined. The American philosopher Charles Sanders Peirce (1839–1914) "now recognized as the most original and the most versatile intellect that the Americas have so far produced") [69] made precisely that point:

> If I had a son, I should instill into him this view of morality (that is that Ethics is the science of the method of bringing Self-Control to bear to gain satisfaction) and [help] him to see that there is but one thing that raises one individual above another—Self-Mastery; and [I] should teach him that the Will is Free only in the sense that, by employing the proper appliances, he can make himself behave in the way he really desires to behave. As to what one ought to desire, it is, *I should show him . . . to make his life beautiful, admirable. Now the science of the Admirable is true Esthetics* [emphasis added].[70]

In this context and others, one of our research-based[71] Tutor Comments introduces students to a fundamental question that typically inspires a limbic response: *In the definition of your goals, ask yourself: "is it beautiful?"*

---

69   Peirce is described in Encyclopedia Britannica as "the most original and the most versatile intellect that the Americas have so far produced." See also Nubiola, Jaime and Barrena, Sara "Charles Peirce's First Visit to Europe, 1870-71" *European Journal of Pragmatism and American Philosophy* I-1/2 (2009)

70   Peirce, Charles cited in Oakes, Edward, "Discovering the American Aristotle" *First Things*, December 1993.

71   See Diessner, Rhett, Iyer, Ravi, Smith, Meghan M., and Haidt, Jonathan, "Who engages with moral beauty?" *Journal of Moral Education* 42(2), 2013, 139–163. The abstract states, in part:

> Aristotle considered moral beauty to be the *telos* of human virtues. Displays of moral beauty have been shown to elicit the moral emotion of elevation and cause a desire to become a better person and to engage in prosocial behavior. Study 1 ($N = 5380$) shows engagement with moral beauty is related to several psychological constructs relevant to moral education, and structural models reveal that the story of engagement with moral beauty may be considered a story of love and connectedness; it is uniquely predictive of caring for, being empathic of, loving, and valuing benevolence toward others . . . . Convergent with other research showing that moral emotions motivate moral behavior, we suggest that moral education programs increase their focus on developing engagement with moral beauty . . . .

AN AIS TUTOR COMMENT FREQUENTLY SHARED WITH STUDENTS: "IS IT BEAUTIFUL?"

Charles Darwin would suggest that the inherent sociability in human nature bends our perception of beauty toward "sympathy" and the capacity to love. Mengzi likewise referred to the potential "goodness" and "beauty" of the human mind. And Aristotle suggested our best and highest aim is "a beautiful life." He wrote:

> *If all people competed for the beautiful, and strained to do the most beautiful things, everything people need in common, and the greatest good for each in particular, would be achieved....*[72]

The philosopher Immanuel Kant echoed all three of these perspectives in his "Critique of Practical Reason" --also repeated on his tombstone: *"Two things fill the mind with ever new and increasing admiration and awe... the starry heavens above me and the moral law within me."*[73] The "moral law" that inspired Kant was seen as an attribute of reason in human nature--not an external demand from a divine source.

Darwin, Mengzi, Aristotle, and Kant are four of the most admired thinkers in history. All support asking yourself an elegantly simple question: *In the definition of your goals, ask yourself: "Is it beautiful?"*

---

72   Aristotle, *Nicomachean Ethics* (Sachs, trans.; 2002), p. 173.

73   See https://www.departments.bucknell.edu/history/carnegie/kant/tomb.html (Bucknell University site).

AIS educational Interventions that blend emotion and cognition: Impact of the Abraham Lincoln and Frederick Douglass assignments.

Introducing students to admirable lives and transformative ideas fosters learning through a blend of emotion and cognition. The limbic brain feels an *emotional* connection with a potential role model and *cognition* allows students to identify which personal qualities and ideas are worthy of emulation and habituation.

AIS follows this pedagogy, in part, by asking students to complete a "Gratitude Statement" (see Chapter 2), and in assignments or tutor comments highlighting the lives and work of:

- Two individuals previously held as slaves who became world-historical thinkers (Frederick Douglass and Epictetus)
- Six prominent philosophers (Mengzi, Plato, Aristotle, Martha Nussbuam, Sissela Bok, and Albert Camus)
- Two former Presidents of the United States (Abraham Lincoln and Barack Obama)
- One Roman Emperor (Marcus Aurelius)
- One former President of South Africa (Nelson Mandela)
- Two psychiatrists who saw the best and worst in humanity during the Holocaust (Viktor Frankl and Roberto Assagioli)
- Two scientists who thought deeply about the aims and methodology of science (Charles Darwin and Richard Feynman)

As evidenced by thousands of AIS student answers and hundreds of related comments, these diverse figures are deemed worthy of emulation because they exhibited *purpose driven* lives grounded on empathy and focused on truth-seeking and truth telling in building a more admirable world.

Our longest combined assignment, which focused on the lives of Abraham Lincoln and Frederick Douglass, was explicitly designed to elicit both limbic and cognitive responses. Both men experienced levels of hardship unlike anything most contemporary young people have encountered.[74] Still, students resonate with stories about resilience in the past because their experience in the present has produced record levels of anxiety and depression.[75]

FOUR AIS STUDENT COMMENTS ABOUT THE IMPACT OF THE ABRAHAM LINCOLN AND FREDERICK DOUGLASS ASSIGNMENTS:

[1] Shenk's article, "Lincoln's Great Depression," was both eye-opening and comforting. I continuously battle my own mental wars daily. Sometimes I win and other times I lose. Knowing that a highly respected individual like Abraham Lincoln went through similar struggles provides me with the inspiration I need to continue.

[2] Douglass's speeches really resonated with me because he held truth and compassion in each word he said, and I want to utilize that in my life. I want to inspire others through my purpose and through my intention, to make sure that the legacy I leave behind inspires others because I am passionate and honest, and the work that I have done backs up my claims.

[3] The Lincoln/Douglass readings were a major influence on changes in my answer. This was mostly because I found them somewhat relatable, especially the ones

---

74   The depth of Lincoln's impoverished childhood was described by historian Doris Kearns Goodwin in her book *Leadership In Turbulent Times*, 2018, p. 4:

When Abraham was nine, [his mother] Nancy Hanks died from what was known as milk sickness, a disease transmitted by way of cows that had eaten poisonous plants. After her burial, Thomas [Lincoln] abandoned his young son and his twelve-year-old daughter, Sarah, for a period of seven months while he returned to Kentucky to find a new wife. They were left on their own in what Lincoln described as "a wild region," a nightmarish place where "the panther's scream filled the night with fear and bears preyed on the swine." When Abraham's new stepmother, Sarah Bush Johnston, returned with Thomas, she found the children living like animals — "wild — ragged & dirty." She was stunned to find that the floorless cabin lacked even a door. Inside, there were few furnishings, no beds, and scant bedding.

75   See relevant data and discussion in Chapter Two ("Gratitude") under the subtitle "Gratitude, human connection, and mental Health."

about Lincoln. I say somewhat relatable because I felt that Lincoln and I faced the same problems, mentally speaking, but we took different paths. I took a path where I was unconfident and dishonest. Whereas Lincoln decided to take a path where he was true to his convictions and had the courage, to be honest. These readings made me reflect on why I took my road and why he took his. My conclusion was that we had different standards and goals for ourselves. I took my road of dishonesty because I was afraid of failure and how I looked to others. He took his road because he wanted to make a real difference in the world. He stayed true to himself and sought to correct the wrong in the world. Meanwhile, I crumbled to others' opinions and views about me. Ultimately, I lost faith in myself.

[4] Douglass demonstrates outstanding moral character in his speeches. He advocates for universal human rights and a more ethical society. His convictions show his integrity, leadership skills, and compassion for others. In "The Composite Nation," he writes, "Trust is the foundation of society. Where there is no truth, there can be no trust, and where there is no trust there can be no society." His integrity is shown through his argument....

CHAPTER FOUR

TRUST

Trust is the foundation of society.... where there is no trust there can be no society.

-- Frederick Douglass, *A Composite Nation* (1867)

What is trust?

The dictionary definition of trust indicates reliance on the "character, ability, strength, or truth of someone or something." [1] Trust is when we don't have to continuously check and recheck whether someone will treat us properly; we *trust* they will act in accordance with reasonable expectations.

We trust strangers with our lives everyday. Consider any large building you enter. Look up at the ceiling. There will likely be tons of steel and concrete directly above your head--placed there by the lowest bidder. Your safety *at that moment* depends upon the integrity of the architects, suppliers, and workers who built the building. [2]

Understanding the social and personal importance of trust

A small number of AIS students have told us they were enthralled by the story of *The Wolf of Wall Street* (a 2013 film depicting the life of Jordan Belfort, convicted of securities fraud and money laundering). One wrote:

---

1   "Trust" Merriam-Webster (2022).

2   This theme is also developed in the Appendix: "Friendship, Fidelity and Academic Integrity."

> *[T]hose who cheat tend to get ahead. For example, the movie "Wolf of Wall Street," starring Leonardo DiCaprio, promotes cheating the stock system to become rich and successful. . . . These rich, successful men who cheated to get to the top are respected and therefore trusted.*

We think the student who wrote that observation was confused by the origins and meaning of trust. Our job as educators is to offer a competing narrative--also relevant to building a *community of trust* on college campuses. Former Federal Reserve Chairman Alan Greenspan provided such a narrative in a 1999 Harvard commencement speech,[3] now featured in an AIS assignment. [4] His emphasis on the social and personal importance of trust echoed views of thinkers as diverse as Frederick Douglass and Adam Smith.

The economic value of trust

Economist Tim Hartford describes what a simple transaction of buying milk would look like without basic societal trust:

> Imagine going to the corner store to buy a carton of milk, only to find that the refrigerator is locked. When you've persuaded the shopkeeper to retrieve the milk, you then end up arguing over whether you're going to hand the money over first, or whether he is going to hand over the milk. Finally, you manage to arrange an elaborate simultaneous exchange. A little taste of life in a world without trust — now imagine trying to arrange a mortgage.[5]

Hartford further explains just how valuable trust has become in the modern economy:

> "If you take a broad enough definition of trust, then it would explain basically all the difference between the per capita

---

3   Greenspan, Alan, Remarks by Chairman Alan Greenspan: Commencement address at Harvard University, Cambridge, Massachusetts, June 10, 1999. http://bit.ly/41aZ3rP.

4   The Academic Integrity Seminar includes the following exercise:

Please read a Harvard commencement speech by former Federal Reserve Board Chairman Alan Greenspan (1999) and answer the following question: *Do you think Greenspan is being realistic or naive about the possibility of business ethics?*

5   Hartford, Tim, "The Economics of Trust," *Forbes*, September 25, 2006.

income of the United States and Somalia," ventures Steve Knack, a senior economist at the World Bank who has been studying the economics of trust for over a decade. That suggests that trust is worth $12.4 trillion dollars a year to the U.S., which, in case you are wondering, is 99.5% of this country's income.[6]

Greenspan pointed out in his Harvard commencement speech: *"Trust is at the root of any economic system based on mutually beneficial exchange. In virtually all transactions, we rely on the word of those with whom we do business. Were this not the case, exchange of goods and services could not take place on any reasonable scale."*

The qualities that Frederick Douglass displays as a thinker and a writer are that he is very honest.... He said, "Mankind is not held together by lies. Trust is the foundation of society. Where there is no truth, there can be no trust, and where there is no trust there can be no society." I think he is correct that there has to be some kind of trust in society because without it the nation would go into chaos and the good in people would be completely gone.

-- AIS student comment

The Prisoner's Dilemma

A well-known example of trust in game theory is the "Prisoner's Dilemma." The following description was provided by the *Stanford Encyclopedia of Philosophy*:

[Two individuals] have been arrested for robbing [a bank] and placed in separate isolation cells. Both care much more about their personal freedom than about the welfare of their

---

6   Hartford, Tim, "The Economics of Trust," *Forbes*, September 25, 2006.

accomplice. A clever prosecutor makes the following offer to each: "You may choose to confess or remain silent. If you confess and your accomplice remains silent I will drop all charges against you and use your testimony to ensure that your accomplice does serious time. Likewise, if your accomplice confesses while you remain silent, they will go free while you do the time. If you both confess I get two convictions, but I'll see to it that you both get early parole. If you both remain silent, I'll have to settle for token sentences on firearms possession charges. If you wish to confess, you must leave a note with the jailer before my return tomorrow morning."[7]

Summary of the prisoners' options

- Cooperate with each other by staying silent. In this context the prosecutor would have to settle for "token sentences on firearms possession charges."

- One prisoner confesses: If one prisoner confesses while the other remains silent, the prisoner who confesses will go free. The prisoner who remains silent will do "serious time."

- Both prisoners confess: Both prisoners will face a lengthy sentence, but the prosecutor promises "early parole" for each.

If only the prisoners could trust each other to keep quiet!

A metaphor for trust

The Prisoner's Dilemma can also be used as a metaphor for trust more generally. Every day, we encounter situations where there is incentive to defect and take advantage of other people. Going back to Tim Hartford's example of buying milk without trust, both the customer and the shop owner could defect and cheat the other. The owner could take the money and tell the customer to get out of the store. The customer could steal the milk and never come back. Both of those outcomes represent a loss of value to the larger society.

---

7   "Prisoner's Dilemma," *Stanford Encyclopedia of Philosophy* (revised April 2, 2019).

Trust or Cheat?

	Trust	Cheat
Trust	Customer buys the milk	Customer steals the milk
Cheat	Store owner steals the money	Nobody buys any milk

We repeatedly encounter this incentive structure in our daily lives. We'd be better off finding ways to be the Trust-Trust box as much as we can, because we can do so much more together if I trust you and you trust me. A lack of trust creates an inability to work and live together.

Trust or Cheat?

	Trust	Cheat
Trust	We both win	I cheat you
Cheat	You cheat me	We both lose

Research by evolutionary biologist Robert Axelrod [8] shows that trust emerges in *repeated* prisoner's dilemmas. When repeated prisoner's dilemma exercises are played among a variety of competing game theory strategies, "Tit for Tat" emerges as a top-performing strategy-- i.e., starting out trusting and then mimicking the other player after that, trusting them if they trust and defecting if they defect. In other words: *Trust, but don't be a sucker.*

---

8   Axelrod, Robert, *The Evolution of Cooperation,* 2006.

Much of modern rules, ethics, and culture are about instilling trust across a society. As Greenspan suggested to his Harvard audience, the most universal ethical principle of all--the Golden Rule--is fundamentally about instilling trust in interactions with others. "Treat others the way you would want to be treated" is a coordination mechanism for getting in the Trust-Trust box.

The "practical virtue" of trust

Alan Greenspan also suggested that business ethics was a "practical virtue" that can add value to companies:

> *And beyond the personal sense of satisfaction, having a reputation for fair dealing is a profoundly practical virtue. We call it "good will" in business and add it to our balance sheets.*

The goodwill built by businesses is based on their reputation for integrity. When I buy a product from Costco, I'm not worried I'll be stuck with unreturnable defective goods. I know Costco has a liberal return policy. That's *value-added* by being trustworthy, not naive.

Many students (and faculty!) think of businesses as fundamentally self-interested, so much so that they're willing to take advantage of consumers to make an extra buck. But what happens to companies that repeatedly behave that way? Do their dissatisfied customers come back? Do you use the car mechanic again that overcharged you last time? Quite the opposite. We seek out businesses that we trust. We seek employees, team members, and colleagues whom we trust. Why? Because it is not possible to work productively with people, businesses, or organizations we don't trust.

Greenspan acknowledged that not everyone is trustworthy, but pointed out the benefit of achieving success by honest means:

> *I do not deny that many appear to have succeeded in a material way by cutting corners and manipulating associates, both in their professional and in their personal lives. But material success is possible in this world and far more satisfying when it comes without*

> *exploiting others. The true measure of a career is to be able to be content, even proud, that you succeeded through your own endeavors without leaving a trail of casualties in your wake.*

Success matters, but honest success matters more. Economist Russ Roberts wrote in this regard about the torment that ponzi-schemer Bernie Madoff must have felt while his scheme was deceiving trusted investors:

> *For years, financial advisor Bernie Madoff was seen by the outside world as a financial genius whose acumen and foresight improbably allowed him to earn consistently high returns for the investors who trusted him . . . . But Madoff knew that he was a fraud. He knew he wasn't lovely. His returns and promises came not from his ability and skill as an investor but from his ability and skill to deceive.* [9]

Ultimately, Greenspan made four points about trust:

[1] Trust is central to successful economic systems

[2] Trust is grounded on the universal ethical principle of reciprocity

[3] A reputation for trustworthiness is a "practical virtue" that enhances prospects for economic success

[4] Relationships grounded on trust promote personal happiness

Why do students resonate with Alan Greenspan's Harvard Commencement speech?

It's fascinating to wonder why most students respond positively to Greenspan's Harvard commencement speech. After all, even as an iconic (and sometimes controversial) figure to older generations, Greenspan gave the speech before many contemporary college students were born.

Here are three anonymous examples from student seminar responses during 2022 (the full list going back to 2006 is much, much longer!):

---

9   Roberts, Russ, *How Adam Smith Can Change Your Life: An Unexpected Guide to Human Nature and Happiness* (2015), p. 44.

Like Greenspan once said, "material success is possible in this world and far more satisfying when it comes without exploiting others." This quote influenced my thinking a lot. It made me understand that I have a responsibility to treat everyone fairly, have a responsibility to care about the community, and have a responsibility to build the world. Just living for myself is not enough, I need to live for more good purposes.

--AIS student comment

There is little satisfaction in life through cheating, and reading the speech that Greenspan stated to the Harvard graduates really resonated with me. You get out what you put in and cutting corners will get me nowhere. I deeply regret being dishonest with my academic work, and this seminar has helped begin those thought processes and start becoming an improved student with newfound goals.

-- AIS student comment

Greenspan's outlook on business ethics really moved [me] in a way that I did not expect. As a business major, seeing the way that he wanted to pursue [a] career in business has made me realize that I need to change some of the ways that I planned on approaching my upcoming career.

-- AIS student comment

Greenspan anticipated technological developments that occurred in students' lifetimes. The relationships of trust that used to exist in small towns and villages are now replicated on a massive scale through social media. For example, would you frequent a restaurant where the restaurant owners had established a social media reputation of being dishonest? Or would you purchase a product on Amazon that had multiple reviews for being defective? Now more than ever, businesses must earn and maintain the trust of their customers.

Students in this generation have grown up with their entire lives documented digitally. They know that what you say and do can follow you for a lifetime. From high school social media to online shopping to "X" handles, one's reputation is a cumulation of hundreds of interactions over time. So it makes sense that students can see how reputation would matter if they are trying to succeed in a career or in business.

Much of modern rules, ethics, and culture are about instilling trust across a society. As Greenspan suggested to his Harvard audience, the most universal ethical principle of all--the Golden Rule--is fundamentally about instilling trust in interactions with others.

The Trust Journal

Most students see Greenspan's point right away: *integrity builds trust, and trust contributes to success in life.* But some remain skeptical. For those students, AIS tutors sometimes include a second exercise, *The Trust Journal:*

TRUST IDENTIFICATION EXERCISE

On any single day of your choice, please keep a written log of occasions when you trusted others (a person, design, product, or service) and others trusted you. Keep your Trust Identification Journal in two categories:

- *Instances where you trusted others*

- *Instances where others trusted you*

Here are three examples:

- *I trusted my morning coffee was not toxic or poisonous.*

- *When I drove to work, I trusted other drivers to drive responsibly.*

- *While at work, my colleagues trusted me to share information accurately and honestly.*

Question 1: In addition to recording occasions when you trusted others, please note any instance when others broke trust with you. What emotions did you feel?

Question 2: Would you regard it as a betrayal of trust if a teacher announced an examination date and then (without warning) gave the examination several days early? Explain.

Question 3: How do you think most teachers feel when students betray trust by engaging in academic dishonesty? Explain.

This exercise works because it asks students to turn the value of trust inward: *Who do I trust and who trusts me?* Once they understand the vast amount of trust occurring in daily life, they can appreciate how impactful breaches of trust can be. We all remember when a friend or colleague betrayed our trust; it's a horrible feeling and cannot easily be repaired.

No one suggests trust occurs from moral righteousness alone. Society depends on regulations, culture, custom, values, and mutual reinforcement of those values for us to land in the "Trust-Trust" box as a societal steady state. "I trust you, so you trust me" is much better than "I distrust you, so you distrust me." We want students to see--as stated in the overview of an Oxford University study--that "generalized trust is a valuable social resource, not only for the individual but for the wider society as well."[10]

---

10   Noah, Carl and Billari, Francesco C, Plos-One "Generalized Trust and Intelligence in the United States" (2014).

Truth-telling and Professional Responsibility

To be qualified to practice law … a person must be of good moral character … Good moral character includes 'qualities of honesty, fairness, candor, [and] trustworthiness ….'

--from In re Stephen Glass, California Supreme Court, (2014)

————————

You will make mistakes. Try not to make big ones …. A simple error in reporting a conclusion will be forgiven if publicly corrected. But never, ever will fraud be forgiven. The penalty is professional death, exile, never again to be trusted.

— E. O. Wilson, Pellegrino University Research Professor at Harvard University and winner of the National Medal of Science (*Letters to a Young Scientist*, 2013)

Why teach professional ethics to college students?
We encourage students to think about professional ethics even if they haven't decided on a career path. Our aim is to foster insights and habits that will serve them well in whatever career they pursue. AIS exercises in this regard are among the most popular with seminar students for reasons stated in the following student comment:

> *[Before taking the seminar], I thought that the most important quality in the workplace is the dedication to work. However, after going through the assigned readings, exercises, and watching the [Shattered Glass] movie, I understood that integrity is the most important quality in the workplace because honesty and loyalty to our coworkers and employer will enable us to build trusting and long-lasting relationships and success in our careers.*

Nearly every profession has an ethics code that was developed through consensus, refined over time, and forms the baseline for acceptable conduct. These codes necessarily reflect customization for mores particular to the field. For example, the *Code of Ethics for Nurses* emphasizes the respect for human dignity and primacy of the patient's interests,[1] while the *Code of Ethics for Professional Engineers* directs engineers to "adhere to the principles of sustainable development in order to protect the environment for future generations." [2] However, at the core of most professional codes of ethics are common principles including *honesty, integrity, reciprocity,* and *personal accountability.*

Learning to identify relevant ethical standards will help students prepare for workplace environments where they need a default position about how to respond to an ethical challenge. There may not be time for protracted analysis ("should I lie to the judge or not?"). The importance of this effort was stated by Derek Bok, past-president of Harvard University:

> Schools of law, business, and medicine have all been criticized repeatedly for failing to convey the values and ideals that should animate their respective professions and practitioners. However difficult the task, any faculty concerned about the

---

1   American Nurses Association, *Code of Ethics for Nurses With Interpretive Statements* (2015) https://bit.ly/3rmfchy.

2   National Society of Professional Engineers, *NSPE Code of Ethics for Professional Engineers* (July 2019): https://bit.ly/3r0cEGv.

well-being of its graduates ought to provide students with some vision of this kind, so that they can ponder it and think how it could help to guide their own careers.[3]

Ethics in the legal profession: The case of Peter Cannon

AIS students are asked to consider a 2010 judicial holding [4] pertaining to Peter Cannon, a lawyer who plagiarized a brief submitted in a bankruptcy proceeding. The Iowa Supreme Court summarized the infraction and sanctioned Cannon with a career-damaging "public reprimand:"

> [A lower court judge in a bankruptcy proceeding], having found Cannon's briefs to be of unusually high quality, issued an order directing Cannon to certify that he was the author of the two briefs in question. Cannon filed a response indicating that both briefs were his sole responsibility and that they "relied heavily" upon an article entitled *Why Professionals Must be Interested in "Disinterestedness" Under the Bankruptcy Code* by William H. Schrag and Mark C. Haut. Cannon further admitted that his initial brief "exceeded permissible fair use without attestation" of the source. He reported he had informed his client about his mistake as well as the bar association.

> The bankruptcy court . . . concluded that seventeen of the nineteen pages of legal analysis in the initial brief were verbatim excerpts from the article, with only variations for format and deletion of matters detrimental to Cannon's position . . . .

The Court then provided a case comparison and sanction determination:

> In *Iowa Supreme Court Board of Professional Ethics & Conduct v. Lane,* 642 N.W.2d 296 (Iowa 2002), we addressed the question of whether plagiarism constituted an ethical violation. In *Lane,* the attorney submitted a post-trial brief in federal court that was largely plagiarized from a treatise. Just as in this case, a federal

---

3   Derek Bok, "College and the Well-Lived Life," *Chronicle of Higher Education,* January 31, 2010.

4   Iowa Supreme Court Attorney Disciplinary Board v. Cannon, No. 10-0520, October 15, 2010.

> judge asked Lane to certify the author or authors of the brief. Unlike this case, however, Lane did not immediately acknowledge the plagiarism and failed to respond to the court for several months. When Lane did respond, he buried the plagiarized treatise in a four-page, single-spaced list of sources . . . .
>
> In *Lane*, we suspended the attorney's license for six months . . . . It is clear, however, that *Lane* represents a more egregious case than this proceeding. In *Lane*, the attorney not only committed plagiarism, but attempted to conceal that misconduct from the court. Further, in *Lane*, we found that the attorney charged an excessive fee. Neither an effort of concealment nor an excessive fee is present in this case. Yet, Cannon copied extensive portions of the Schrag and Haut article and omitted unfavorable passages of it. This is misrepresentation, plain and simple . . . .
>
> Under all the facts and circumstances, we conclude that a public reprimand is the appropriate sanction in this matter.

The court in the *Cannon* decision identified aggravating factors in the *Lane* case that merited a stronger sanction. Students often see parallels to academic dishonesty proceedings, including favorable consideration given to individuals who do not seek to hide or justify a violation.

Finally, AIS tutors want students to understand the importance of a "public reprimand" in any profession.[5] They need to know that federal privacy rights enacted to protect their "education records" do not apply to disciplinary proceedings in subsequent careers and professions. Indeed, as highlighted in the Ethics in Scientific Research section of this chapter, open disclosure of professional wrongdoing may be deemed in the public interest.

Students frequently comment on the usefulness of the Cannon case exercise:

---

5   AIS alerts students to a policy enforced by the Florida Supreme Court: *"The public reprimand is a Supreme Court ordered form of public discipline that declares the conduct of the lawyer improper. Public reprimands are by publication, in some cases by appearance before the 52 member Florida Bar Board of Governors and are public"* Additional discussion can be found at the *Florida Bar Journal Post*: "The Goal of the Public Reprimand: Rehabilitation" (2008).

> *I think the reading about [courts punishing] plagiarism among lawyers really influenced my thinking. For me, it was a great example of a real way that academic integrity issues can affect your lives outside of school and could alter your entire career and professional life. Although I did realize the severity of plagiarism and cheating within the academic realm, [the reading] helped to solidify these feelings outside of a strictly school context.*

Our Cannon case assignment allows us to highlight the fact that the legal profession has long established formal and informal codes of ethics going back to the 13th century. An overview was provided by law professor Carol Rice Andrews (internal footnotes omitted):

> The first set of ABA [American Bar Association] model standards – the 1908 Canons of Ethics 4 – was largely a verbatim restatement of the 1887 Alabama State Bar Association Code of Ethics. The 1887 Alabama Code itself relied upon leading nineteenth century authorities, and they in turn built upon earlier works. This evolution continues back to at least thirteenth century Europe, where lawyers took oaths to abide by a list of ethical precepts. When viewed in isolation, any one of these historical sets of standards may seem quite different than a set from another era, but when viewed in context of their broader 800-year evolution, the standards are remarkably similar over time. *The core concepts – litigation fairness, competence, loyalty, confidentiality, reasonable fees, and public service – have remained surprisingly constant.* To be sure, modern codes have made significant advances, but the primary changes have come in the degree of detail and the regulatory effect of the standards of conduct, not in the core duties [emphasis added].[6]

---

6   Andrews, Carol Rice, Standards of Conduct for Lawyers: An 800-Year Evolution, 57 SMU L. Rev. 1385 at 1386-87 (2004).

Each state's bar association has adopted codes of ethical conduct based largely on the American Bar Association's (ABA) *Model Rules of Professional Conduct*. [7] Several of the ABA Model Rules establish standards that are relevant not only to legal practice, but to intellectual and personal integrity generally, including the following:

- Rule 3.3: Candor Toward the Tribunal – This rule not only prohibits lawyers from knowingly "mak[ing] a false statement of fact or law to a tribunal" and "offer[ing] evidence that the lawyer knows is false," but also requires lawyers to "correct a false statement of material fact or law previously made to the tribunal by the lawyer" and to disclose legal authority that is "directly adverse to the position of [their] client" if opposing counsel fails to disclose it. [8]

- Rule 3.4: Fairness to Opposing Party & Counsel – In the context of a judicial proceeding, this rule sets the ground rules for dealing with the other side, prohibiting a lawyer from "falsify[ing] evidence, counsel[ing] or assist[ing] a witness to testify falsely," destroying evidence, and other actions that may impede conduct of a fair trial. [9]

- Rule 4.1: Truthfulness in Statements to Others – When representing a client, a lawyer may not make a false statement or fail to disclose a material fact when interacting with a third party (non-client). [10]

- Rule 6.1: Voluntary Pro Bono Publico Service – Stating, "Every lawyer has a professional responsibility to provide legal services to those unable to pay," this rule sets an annual target of 50 hours of free legal services to "persons of limited means" and "charitable, religious, civic, community, governmental and educational organizations in matters that are designed primarily to address the needs of persons of limited means." [11]

7   Available at https://bit.ly/3tal0eO.

8   Available at https://bit.ly/46aejIm.

9   Available at https://bit.ly/3LCbCa9.

10   Available at https://bit.ly/3EXrpN3.

11   Available at https://bit.ly/3VLXv7Y.

Suspected violations of a legal code of ethics are generally referred to state bar and attorney grievance commissions. Students may observe parallels to the student conduct system (also administered by peers) and range of penalties (which may also result in suspension or expulsion).

Ethics in Journalism: The Case of Stephen Glass

One of our most appreciated Seminar assignments is watching the film *Shattered Glass*.[12] The film dramatizes writer Stephen Glass' time at the *New Republic* and the events leading to the discovery of his multiple fabricated news stories.

Glass was a reporter for *The New Republic* between 1995 and 1998. He started as an intern, doing small administrative tasks, but quickly gained a reputation as the "Darth Vader of Detail" with an ability to find colorful characters and incisive anecdotes that amazed fellow writers.[13] Only 25 years old, just a few years after graduating from college, Stephen Glass appeared to be a gifted journalist. He was, in fact, a gifted liar. The colorful characters and anecdotes that filled his stories were largely imaginary. It was, in the words of a friend and writer at *The New Republic*, "the most elaborate fraud in journalistic history."[14] The true extent of his fraud wasn't known until an editor confronted Glass about a news story describing meetings that did not happen, people who did not exist, and a company that was only a figment of Glass' imagination. An investigation ultimately found that 27 articles he wrote—more than half of the articles he wrote for the *New Republic*—included fabrications.

Glass's actions flagrantly violated any number of ethical precepts, including a professional code of ethics for journalists. The 2014 Society of Professional Journalists Code of Ethics (SPJ Code) is contained on a single page with four key principles—*Seek Truth and Report It, Minimize Harm, Act Independently,* and *Be Accountable and Transparent.*[15] Additional guidance for journalists is provided within each principle; for example, the principle of accountability and

---

12   Description available at https://rb.gy/rvyya.

13   Bissinger, B., "Shattered Glass," *Vanity Fair,* September 5, 2007.

14   Rosin, H., "Hello, My Name Is Stephen Glass, and I'm Sorry," *The New Republic,* November 10, 2014,

15   Society of Professional Journalists, Code of Ethics (2023): https://www.spj.org/ethicscode.asp

transparency encourages journalists to "acknowledge mistakes and correct them promptly and prominently."

Though not in place while he was working as a journalist, it's hard to imagine the 2014 SPJ Code would have deterred Glass (an earlier version of the Code certainly didn't do so). Once the first fabricated quote had its intended effect, the temptation to fabricate another, and another, became irresistible. His fabricated material was the secret to writing "home run" stories and it weighed on him. Before anybody knew about the fabrications, Glass would wander the office asking colleagues: "are you mad at me?" He asked them so often that one threatened to "whack [him] with a magazine" each time he asked.[16]

The depth and frequency of Glass's deceptions raise tough questions. How did they metastasize from isolated instances of embellishment to entirely fake articles supported by fake notes, phone calls, and websites? And for the people to whom Glass later apologized, were the apologies sincere or another hoax? The director of the film *Shattered Glass* once met Glass at a party where Glass expressed contrition, but the director didn't know if he could believe him: "Glass said everything a person who was contrite would say . . . . Knowing his history, I can hope that was sincere, but that's just hope."[17]

An important goal of the Academic Integrity Seminar is to help students recognize the risks of *habitual deception*. While the instance of deception that landed them in the Seminar is far from an international scandal, the next time they choose to be dishonest, they walk the same path as Glass. We may never know with certainty why Glass chose to fabricate his first story, but the growing extravagance of his lies suggests that he became habituated to dishonesty. It soon became necessary for him to construct ever more elaborate explanations and tell ever more lies to help cover the old ones. Eventually, Glass was lying every day, if not in his "reporting," then to his colleagues and in his public projection of a journalist abiding by professional ethics.

---

16   Rosin, H., "Hello, My Name Is Stephen Glass, and I'm Sorry," *The New Republic,* November 10, 2014,

17   "Postscript: Shattered Glass," *Vanity Fair,* September 5, 2007.

Once the habit of dishonesty is entrenched, as it was with Glass, a monumental scaffolding of lies becomes almost inevitable.

AIS tutors advise students that repeated deception of others can also lead to *deception of the self.* Here's one of our comments:

> You may remember a scene near the end of *Shattered Glass* when the editor of *The New Republic* said to Stephen: *"I just want you to tell me the truth, Steve, can you do that?* The editor was beginning to suspect that Stephen had been lying to others for so long that he was incapable of distinguishing between truth and falsehood. At that moment in the film it became clear that *the greatest victim of Stephen's deception was Stephen himself.*

A related tutor comment cites a famous passage in Dostoevsky's *The Brothers Karamazov.* In this passage an elder in the Eastern Orthodox Christian tradition warns about the long-term risks of self-deception:

> The main thing is that you stop telling lies to yourself. The one who lies to himself and believes his own lies comes to a point where he can distinguish no truth either within himself or around him, and thus enters into a state of disrespect towards himself and others. Respecting no one, he loves no one, and to amuse and divert himself in the absence of love, he gives himself up to his passions and to vulgar delights and becomes a complete animal in his vices, and all of it from perpetual lying to other people and to himself.[18]

In 2014, approximately twenty years after the events at *The New Republic,* the California Supreme Court denied Glass' petition to become an attorney in that state. The Court's opinion revealed that Glass still contended with a lack of trust:

> Glass's journalistic dishonesty was not a single lapse of judgment, which we have sometimes excused, but involved significant deceit sustained unremittingly for a period of years . . . . Glass's deceit also was motivated by professional ambition, betrayed a vicious, mean spirit and a complete lack of compassion for others, along

---

18   Dostoyevsky, Fyodor. *The Brothers Karamazov* (McDuff, trans.; 1996), p.46

with arrogance and prejudice against various ethnic groups. In all these respects, his misconduct bore directly on his character in matters that are critical to the practice of law.[19]

Glass' dishonesty in 2002-2004 New York State bar proceedings may have colored the Court's view of his conduct during the subsequent California state bar hearing process--which the Court thought was tainted with "hypocrisy and evasiveness." [20] The Court observed:

> [Glass] went through many verbal twists and turns at the hearing to avoid acknowledging the obvious fact that in his [earlier] New York bar application he exaggerated his level of assistance to the magazines that had published his fabrications, and that he omitted from his New York bar list of fabrications some that actually could have injured real persons.[21]

Glass's story illustrates the life-long risks associated with habitual lying and self-deception. Read in conjunction with the Iowa Supreme Court decision in the *Cannon* case, AIS students gain immediate, real-world insight into why colleges and universities seek to prepare them for a world in which professional misconduct can be documented and long-remembered.

The Shattered Glass *film made a huge impact on me …. My main emotions during it were second-hand embarrassment, profound sadness, and disappointment. Each chance Glass had to right his wrongs, he instead chose to dig the hole deeper. I saw some of myself reflected in him and it really put into perspective just how these things can happen. It really made me reevaluate my morals and life decisions, in a good way.*

--AIS student comment

---

19   In re Stephen Randall Glass on Admission. State Bar Ct No. 09-M-11736, January 27, 2014

20   In re Stephen Randall Glass on Admission. State Bar Ct No. 09-M-11736, January 27, 2014

21   In re Stephen Randall Glass on Admission. State Bar Ct No. 09-M-11736, January 27, 2014

Ethics in scientific research

AIS tutors urge students to consider the truth-seeking and truth-telling methodology of science as a component of human flourishing.[22] We suggest that scientific methodology, at heart, is a cooperative endeavor, grounded on a unique combination of imagination,[23] creative doubting,[24] disciplined thinking, unbiased observation, honest reporting,[25] replication, and peer review.[26]

---

22 See Saul Perlmutter, John Campbell, and Robert MacCoun in Third Millennium Thinking: Creating Sense in a World of Nonsense (2024). Science, they conclude, has:

> . . . a phenomenal record of providing insight into — if not answers to — the most confounding questions humans have thought to ask. It has helped us to solve puzzles, address problems, and make better lives over millennia. It is a culture of inquiry rooted in the dawn of humankind, with centuries of practice in evaluating conflicting information in a baffling world, and in distinguishing what we know from what we don't. Along the way, scientists have learned from both successes and mistakes, breakthroughs and blunders, to refine the tools with which to address new questions and solve new problems. Some of these tools are physical objects, like measurement tools and instruments — from the sextant to supercolliders to quantum computers. *But others are thinking tools — habits of mind, rubrics, approaches, procedures, standards, ideas, principles, stances . . . .* p 4 [emphasis added].

23 See the third paragraph in Richard Feynman's 1965 Nobel Banquet speech:

> *Imagination* reaches out repeatedly trying to achieve some higher level of understanding, until suddenly I find myself momentarily alone before one new corner of nature's pattern of beauty and true majesty revealed [emphasis added].

See also Note 24.

24 Richard Feynman provided an engaging description of science in a series of lectures delivered at The University of Washington (Seattle) in 1963. The lectures are published in The Meaning of It All: Thoughts of a Citizen-Scientist (2005). In the first lecture "The Uncertainty of Science," Feynman stated that:

> Scientists, therefore, are used to dealing with doubt and uncertainty. All scientific knowledge is uncertain. This experience with doubt and uncertainty is important. I believe that it is of very great value, and one that extends beyond the sciences. I believe that to solve any problem that has never been solved before, you have to leave the door to the unknown ajar. You have to permit the possibility that you do not have it exactly right. Otherwise, if you have made up your mind already, you might not solve it . . . . Because we have the doubt, we then propose looking in new directions for new ideas. The rate of the development of science is not the rate at which you make observations alone but, much more important, the rate at which you create new things to test (pp. 26-27).

25 See our discussion in Chapter One about a courageous graduate student who reported a mistake that required retraction of a journal article.

26 Insights from John Moore's book Science as a Way of Knowing (1993) are frequently shared with AIS students in our Tutor comments. Moore (Emeritus Professor of Biology at the University of California-Riverside) wrote that:

> [The methods of science] require disciplined minds capable of accurately recording observations, using data from those observations to develop a tentative explanation (a hypothesis), testing the necessary deductions from that hypothesis, and relating the conclusions . . . to the existing body of scientific information. Not only does the testing of hypotheses make science a self-correcting enterprise, but so does the practice of one scientist testing the conclusions of another. The result is that science is the most powerful mechanism we have for obtaining confirmable information about the natural world . . . . (p. 504).

See also the topic "Scientific Method" in the Stanford Encyclopedia of Philosophy.

> *[T]hinking tools [of science] … encourage us to correct for our own blind spots, biases, and limitations, and to persist even when problems seem unsolvable. They also reflect centuries of wisdom about the essential value — even the necessity — of collaboration, particularly with people who see things differently.*[27]
>
> -- Saul Perlmutter, John Campbell, and Robert MacCoun, *Third Millennium Thinking: Creating Sense in a World of Nonsense* (2024).

Precursors to contemporary science can be found in different cultural traditions.[28] A fully developed methodology of science, however, is a relatively recent development. [29] For example, Einstein's predictions about the distorted locations of stars as a result of the Sun's gravity were famously put to the test during a 1919 solar eclipse. And when Einstein turned out to be right, a breathless *New York Times* headline reported the news: "Light's All Askew in the Heavens, Men of Science

---

27 Perlmutter, Saul, Campbell, John, and MacCoun, Robert, Third Millennium Thinking: Creating Sense in a World of Nonsense (2024), p.3.

28 Philosophical skepticism in Greece is one prominent example, along with Socrates' frequent protestations of ignorance (see our discussion in Chapter Three). Consider also the role of Buddhism identified in Chapter Six, especially the importance of engaging in "right talk" and "mak[ing] sure that whatever you said was worth saying: 'reasoned, accurate, clear and beneficial . . .'" (cited in Armstrong, Karen, Buddha, 2004, p. 70-71). The full reference from Armstrong's book is repeated here:

> Instead of simply avoiding violence, an aspirant must behave gently and kindly to everything and everyone; he must cultivate thoughts of loving-kindness to counter any incipient feelings of ill will. It was very important not to tell lies, but it was also crucial to engage in "right talk" and make sure that whatever you said was worth saying: "reasoned, accurate, clear and beneficial . . . ." *Once this "skillful" behavior became so habitual that it was second nature, the aspirant, Gotama believed, would "feel within himself a pure joy,"* similar to if not identical with the bliss that he had felt as a boy under the rose-apple tree [emphasis added]

More examples can be seen in a useful Wikipedia summary: History of the Scientific Method. None of these early traditions, however, articulated what we now regard as a fully developed scientific method.

29 Even during the late Renaissance, religious authorities in Europe were banning the works of towering scientific figures such as Copernicus and Galileo. Galileo, brought before the inquisition in 1633, and threatened with torture, "disavowed his belief in a revolving earth," but was reportedly heard to mutter *"E pur si muove"* ("and yet it does move") as he left. See Manchester, William, *A World Lit Only by Fire: The Medieval Mind and the Renaissance - Portrait of an Age* (1993), Kindle location 2069, and Livio, Mario, "Did Galileo Truly Say, 'And Yet It Moves'? A Modern Detective Story," *Scientific American*, May 6, 2020.

More or Less Agog Over Results of Eclipse Observations." [30] The excitement in that headline highlighted the novelty of the process as much as the substance of the findings.

Disciplined minds focused on seeking confirmable evidence are hard to find now, let alone in prior eras when "[a]t any moment, under any circumstances, a person could be removed from the world of the senses to a realm of magic creatures and occult powers." [31] We introduce AIS students to this perspective so they might appreciate both the importance of scientific inquiry and their responsibility to sustain it.

---

30   "Lights all Askew in the Heavens . . . ." *New York Times*, November 10, 1919.

31   Manchester, William, *A World Lit Only by Fire: The Medieval Mind and the Renaissance - Portrait of an Age* (1993) Kindle locations 1,225 and 1,241. Manchester also wrote:

> Although they called themselves Christians, medieval Europeans were ignorant of the Gospels. The Bible existed only in a language they could not read. The mumbled incantations at Mass were meaningless to them. They believed in sorcery, witchcraft, hobgoblins, werewolves, amulets, and black magic . . . If a lady died, the instant her breath stopped, servants ran through the manor house, emptying every container of water to prevent her soul from drowning, and before her funeral the corpse was carefully watched to prevent any dog or cat from running across the coffin, thus changing her remains into a vampire . . . .

> Everyone also knew—and every child was taught—that the air all around them was infested with invisible, soulless spirits, some benign but most of them evil, dangerous, long-lived, and hard to kill; that among them were the souls of unbaptized infants, ghouls who snuffled out cadavers in graveyards and chewed their bones, water nymphs skilled at luring knights to death by drowning, dracs who carried little children off to their caves beneath the earth, wolfmen—the undead turned into ravenous beasts—and vampires who rose from their tombs at dusk to suck the blood of men, women, or children who had strayed from home. At any moment, under any circumstances, a person could be removed from the world of the senses to a realm of magic creatures and occult powers. Every natural object possessed supernatural qualities.

While the general population was immersed in a world "of magic creatures and occult powers," the Church was focused on condemnation of discoveries by Copernicus and Galileo. See the digital publication "400 Years Ago the Catholic Church Prohibited Copernicanism" (Ohio State University: *Origins*) https://bit.ly/41q5fMX.

A general account of medieval life can be seen in the book *The Family, Sex and Marriage in England, 1500-1800* (1977), pp. 93, 98 by Lawrence Stone (Professor of History at Princeton University):

> The extraordinary amount of casual interpersonal physical and verbal violence, as recorded in legal and other records, shows clearly that at all levels men and women were extremely short-tempered. The most trivial disagreements tended to lead rapidly to blows, and most people carried a potential weapon, if only a knife to cut their meat . . . . The Elizabethan village was a place filled with malice and hatred, its only unifying bond being the occasional episode of mass hysteria, which temporarily bound together the majority in order to persecute and harry the local witch . . . . What is being postulated for the sixteenth and early seventeenth centuries is a society in which a majority of the individuals that composed it found it very difficult to establish emotional ties to any other person. Children were neglected, brutally treated, and even killed; adults treated each other with suspicion and hostility; affect was low and hard to find. To an anthropologist, there would be nothing very surprising about such a society, which closely resembles the Mundugumor in the Twentieth Century as described by Margaret Mead.

*We have to live to-day by what truth we can get to-day,
and be ready to-morrow to call it falsehood.*[32]

--William James, The Journal of Philosophy
Psychology and Scientific methods (1907).

As we suggested in Chapter One (Power of Stories), the human capacity for honesty and truth-telling has been incentivized in many societies, ancient and modern. One of the most memorable examples in this regard can be seen in ancient Olympia, Greece--the site of the Olympic games for over 1,000 years. Travel there today and you can still see signage about bronze statues of Zeus known as *Zanes*. The Zanes were built and paid for with fines imposed on athletes found to have cheated. Each statue included an inscription naming the athlete and their offense. The position of the Zanes along the entryway to the Olympic stadium was intended to serve as a warning to other athletes: *don't cheat lest you forever be memorialized here.* (See our related MEDIUM article: The Educational Benefits of Timely Reminders.) [33]

One warning couplet on a Zane reads:

Here muscles win, and speedy feet,

Not lots of money spent to cheat.

Set up by elians in fear of god

To frighten crooks who win by fraud.[34]

Many AIS students are surprised to learn that comparable forms of punishment exist today. The Office of Research Integrity (ORI) oversees and directs Public Health Service research integrity activities on

---

32   James, William, "Pragmatism's Conception of Truth" *The Journal of Philosophy, Psychology and Scientific Methods,* Vol. 4, No. 6 (Mar. 14, 1907), p. 150.

33   Pavela, Gary, "The Educational Benefit of Timely Reminders," MEDIUM, February 19, 2023.

34   Cited in the Hellenistic World website (August 20, 2012) and Schulenkorf, Nico, *Critical Issues in Global Sport Management* (2016, p. 54). See, generally, Forbes, Clarence, "Crime and Punishment in Greek Athletics," *The Classical Journal* 47(5), February 1952, pp. 170-171, and Shavin, Naomi, "The Ancient History of Cheating in the Olympics," *Smithsonian Magazine,* August 3, 2016.

behalf of the U.S. Secretary of Health and Human Services. ORI regularly posts names and case files of individuals found responsible for research misconduct (modern-day Zanes). In early 2023, the ORI list of scientific misconduct case summaries included the names of 36 researchers with actively imposed administrative actions against them.[35]

For scientists to do their best work, they must be a part of an institution that supports the conveyance of accurate knowledge across generations. A famous expression of this idea came from Isaac Newton: *"if I have seen further, it is by standing on the shoulders of giants."* [36] A less familiar example confirming the same point is the obscurity of Cardinal Nicholas of Cusa. Comparatively few people have heard of the Cardinal, even though he preceded Copernicus and Kepler by a century in questioning received wisdom about the trajectory of planetary orbits and Earth's location at the center of the universe. The Cardinal's obscurity, according to the historian Jacques Barzun, "is a prime example of the truth that before science could prosper, it had to become an institution."[37]

Science is inherently cumulative. There's no way as a researcher I can go back and replicate everything done before me. I have to accept what's published as accurate and then build on that. Finding out something has been fabricated or falsified, that can throw a monkey wrench into a whole research stream.[38]

-- Joseph Rosse, University of Colorado Associate Vice Chancellor of Research Integrity and Compliance

---

35   *Case Summaries | ORI - The Office of Research Integrity* (2023), https://ori.hhs.gov/content/case_summary.

36   The cited letter from Isaac Newton can be viewed at Historical Society of Pennsylvania archives: https://bit.ly/3LLcwBh.

37   Barzun, J., *From Dawn to Decadence: 500 Years of Cultural Triumph and Defeat, 1500 to the Present.* HarperCollins (2000), p. 230.

38   Rosse, Joseph, University of Colorado Associate Vice Chancellor of Research Integrity and Compliance cited in the Boulder, Colorado *Daily Camera,* "CU-Boulder scientists speak out on research misconduct claim" (February 7, 2014).

The importance of understanding science as a tradition was also expressed by Adam Frank, professor of physics and astronomy at the University of Rochester:

> Behind the giant particle accelerators and space observatories, science is a way of behaving in the world. It is, simply put, a tradition. And as we know from history's darkest moments, even the most enlightened traditions can be broken and lost.[39]

AIS tutors suggest to students that the tradition of science includes an awareness of human fallibility (see our discussion in Chapter One about Darwin's "Golden Rule" for cognitive conditioning). The outrageousness of Stephen Glass's deceptions in journalism and the effort he put into sustaining them may convey a sense that honesty is an easier, more natural "resting state" of the human condition. If only that were true. Scientists share with journalists and those in other professions both a truth-seeking orientation *and* a vulnerability to self-deception. No one has stated this insight more concisely than physicist Richard Feynman:

> *The first principle is that you must not fool yourself—and you are the easiest person to fool.*[40]

---

39   Frank, Adam, "Welcome to the Age of Denial," *New York Times*, August 21, 2013.

40   Feynman, Richard, Cargo Cult Science, 1974 Commencement address at the California Institute of Technology.

CHAPTER SIX

Joyfulness, Purpose, and Fulfillment[1]

Imagination reaches out repeatedly trying to achieve some higher level of understanding, until suddenly I find myself momentarily alone before one new corner of nature's pattern of beauty and true majesty revealed. That was my reward…. Then, having fashioned tools to make access easier to the new level, I see these tools used by other men straining their imaginations against further mysteries beyond. There, are my votes of recognition.

--Richard Feynman, 1965 Nobel Banquet Speech

Stoic philosopher Marcus Aurelius on joy as a worthy aim in life
AIS assignments and tutor comments introduce students to the following observation in Marcus's *Meditations:*

> *A man's joy is to do what is proper to man, and man's proper work is kindness to his fellow man, disdain of the movements of the senses, to discern plausible imaginations, to meditate on Universal Nature and the work of her hands.*[2]

There's much to unpack in Marcus's observation:

---

1   Portions of this chapter previously appeared in Gary Pavela's Law and Policy newsletter.

2   Aurelius, Marcus, *Meditations*, Book VIII (26) (Farquharson, trans).

- From a Stoic perspective, joyfulness arises from recognizing and following a universal order or reason (Logos) reflected in the structure of the Universe.[3] A famous Christian statement of faith by Martin Luther King reflects a similar view: *The arc of the moral universe is long but it bends toward justice.*[4]

- Individuals guided by Logos will display kindness, compassion, and devotion to the common good.

- To "disdain the movement of senses" means to forgo transitory pleasures for the joys of reason and loving kindness.

- To "discern plausible imaginations" means to rely on reason and critical thinking to form beliefs and judgments.

- "To meditate on Universal Nature and the work of her hands" means to remain open to awe, wonder, and joy in contemplation of what physicist Richard Feynman described as "nature's pattern of beauty and true majesty revealed."[5]

Critics sometimes suggest that Stoicism lacks a sense of joy. We think the problem is more a matter of style than substance. In different literary hands, Marcus's call to "meditate on Universal Nature and the work of her hands" could produce a compelling poetic interpretation.[6]

---

3   For a related perspective in the sciences, see Einstein, Albert, "The World As I See It." Einstein observed:

> The most beautiful experience we can have is the mysterious. It is the fundamental emotion that stands at the cradle of true art and true science. Whoever does not know it and can no longer wonder, no longer marvel, is as good as dead, and his eyes are dimmed. It was the experience of mystery -- even if mixed with fear -- that engendered religion. A knowledge of the existence of something we cannot penetrate, our perceptions of the profoundest reason and the most radiant beauty, which only in their most primitive forms are accessible to our minds: it is this knowledge and this emotion that constitute true religiosity. In this sense, and only this sense, I am a deeply religious man... I am satisfied with the mystery of life's eternity and with a knowledge, a sense, of the marvelous structure of existence -- *as well as the humble attempt to understand even a tiny portion of the Reason that manifests itself in nature*" [emphasis added].

4   King Jr., Martin Luther, "Remaining Awake Through a Great Revolution," 1965 Commencement address at Oberlin College.

5   Feynman, Richard, 1965 Nobel Banquet Speech.

6   Memorable literary depictions of joy include Dante's "The Divine Comedy" (*Paradiso*; translation and notes by John Ciardi). After failing to climb directly up the "Mount of Joy," Dante takes a long and treacherous route to arrive in the presence of "the Divine Light of Ultimate Truth:"

> I saw within Its depth how It conceives all things in a single volume bound by Love, of which the Universe is the scattered leaves; substance, accident, and their relation so fused that all I say could do no more than yield a glimpse of that bright revelation. I think I saw the universal

There is no beautifier of complexion, or form, or behavior, like the wish to scatter joy and not pain around us. [7]

--Ralph Waldo Emerson

Distinguishing happiness from joy (and why the distinction matters)

Nelson Mandela wrote in his autobiography that "[t]o be the father of a nation is a great honor, but to be the father of a family is a greater joy." [8]

Mandela's use of the word "joy" described a feeling beyond happiness. It transformed individual experience into the highest level of human insight. *New York Times* columnist David Brooks--influenced by the work of theologian Miroslav Volf at Yale University--provided this analysis:

> *Joy tends to involve some transcendence of self. . . . We can help create happiness, but we are seized by joy. We are pleased by happiness, but we are transformed by joy. When we experience joy we often feel we have glimpsed into a deeper and truer layer of reality.*[9] *A narcissist can be happy, but a narcissist can never be joyful, because the surrender of self is the precise thing a narcissist can't do. A narcissist can't even conceive of joy.*[10]

form that binds these things, for as I speak these words *I feel my joy swell* and my spirits warm. Twenty-five centuries since Neptune saw the Argo's keel have not moved all mankind, recalling that adventure, to such awe [Kindle location 23,934; emphasis added].

Translator John Ciardi wrote:

[For Dante] [t]he essence of God is love, i.e., *caritas*, the love of others. With caritas as the essential mood of the Paradiso, no soul can help but rejoice in the joy of all about it. Contrast the state of things in the Inferno: the infernal souls have all refused to accept and to identify themselves with the Divine Love; *each, therefore, is closed into itself, and no soul in Hell can derive any comfort from any other* (see Inferno, V, note to line 102). *Joy finds its increase exactly in being freely given to others.* As Piccarda soon makes clear to Dante, that joy is expressed in Heaven in no way but in the complete identification with God's love [Kindle location: 16,250; emphasis added].

7   Emerson, Ralph Waldo, "The Conduct of Life" (1860), p. 170.

8   Mandela, Nelson, *Long Walk to Freedom: The Autobiography of Nelson Mandela* (1995), p. 600.

9   See Dante's depiction of "the Divine Light of Ultimate Truth" in note 264.

10 Brooks, David, *The Second Mountain: The Quest for a Moral Life* (2020), Kindle locations 288, 295.

Writing about joy rarely captures the actual experience. The following example from Admiral Richard Byrd (an account of working at an Antarctic weather base in 1934) comes close:

> *Took my daily walk at 4 p.m. in 89 [degrees] of frost . . . I paused to listen to the silence . . . . Here were imponderable processes and forces of the cosmos, harmonious and soundless. Harmony, that was it! That was what came out of the silence . . . . It was enough to catch that rhythm, momentarily to be myself a part of it. In that instant I could feel no doubt of man's oneness with the Universe . . . . It was a feeling that transcended reason; that went to the heart of man's despair and found it groundless. The Universe was a cosmos, not a chaos; man was rightfully a part of that cosmos, as were the day or night.*[11]

The self-transcendence identified by Brooks and Byrd can be seen in both religious and secular traditions (e.g., Buddhism, Taoism, transpersonal psychology, and recent research on the power of awe [12]). It was also identified as one of the core lessons learned in the Harvard University "Grant Study" of adult development (see our introduction). Grant study conclusions--routinely shared with students in AIS tutor comments--were reported in a 2017 *Harvard Gazette* article with the evocative title "Good Genes Are Nice, but Joy Is Better." [13] An overview by long-time study Director George E. Vaillant, MD (also

---

11   Byrd, Richard, *Alone* (1958), pp. 62-3, cited by Storr, Anthony, *Solitude* (1989), p. 36.

12   See Keltner, Dacher, *Awe: The New Science of Everyday Wonder and How It Can Transform Your Life* (2023). Keltner wrote that:

> With emotion science turning its attention to the varieties of positive emotion, in 2003 my longtime collaborator at New York University Jonathan Haidt and I worked to articulate a definition of awe. At the time, there were only a few scientific articles on awe (but thousands on fear). There were no definitions of awe to speak of. So we immersed ourselves in the writings of mystics about their encounters with the Divine. We read treatments of the holy, the sublime, the supernatural, the sacred, and "peak experiences" that people might describe with words like "flow," "joy," "bliss," or even "enlightenment." We considered political theorists like Max Weber and their speculations about the passions of mobs whipped up by demagogues. We read anthropologists' accounts of awe in dance, music, art, and religion in faraway, remote cultures. Drawing upon these veins of scholarship, we defined awe as follows: Awe is the feeling of being in the presence of something vast that transcends your current understanding of the world . . . [Kindle location 302].

> Wild awe returns us to a big idea: that we are part of something much larger than the self, one member of many species in an interdependent, collaborating natural world [Kindle location 1,987].

13   Mineo, Liz, "Good genes are nice, but joy is better," *Harvard Gazette*, April 11, 2017.

included in our introduction) was summarized in a 2001 *Harvard Magazine* article:

> [A]lthough it is not easy to change our defenses by ourselves, *chance favors a prepared mind:* "We can start by admiring how other skillful people cope. Then ponder, when things go badly for us, how we might have used self-defeating mechanisms. Lastly, [Vaillant] says, consider this rule of thumb: *"Don't try to think less of yourself, but try to think of yourself less"* [emphasis added].[14]

George Vaillant's observation that "chance favors a prepared mind" highlights the role of discipline and habituation in expanding the capacity for joy. This perspective can be seen, for example, in the neoplatonic philosophy of Plotinus [15] and the teachings of Buddhism. A paragraph in Karen Armstrong's book *Buddha* summarizes the concept:

> Instead of simply avoiding violence, an aspirant must behave gently and kindly to everything and everyone; he must cultivate thoughts of loving-kindness to counter any incipient feelings of ill will. It was very important not to tell lies, but it was also crucial to engage in "right talk" and make sure that whatever you said was worth saying: "reasoned, accurate, clear and beneficial . . . ." Once this "skillful" behavior became so habitual that it was second nature, the aspirant, Gotama believed, would "feel within himself a pure joy," similar to if not identical with the bliss that he had felt as a boy under the rose-apple tree.[16]

Joy in learning

Drew Faust (then President of Harvard University) addressed a provocative question to a faculty audience in 2013:

---

14   Lambert, Craig, "The Talent for Aging Well," *Harvard Magazine*, March-April, 2001. See also Shenk, Joshua Wolf, "What Makes Us Happy," *The Atlantic*, June, 2009.

15   Russell, Bertrand, *A History of Western Philosophy* (1967), p. 288.

16   Armstrong, Karen, *Buddha* (2004), pp. 70-71. Consider the cited passage in connection with an observation from Marcus Aurelius featured in our Introduction: *"[t]he things you think about determine the quality of your mind. Your soul takes on the color of your thoughts."*

How do we—we who have devoted our lives to scholarship and teaching—how do we affirm and transmit the value—and the excitement—of learning for its own sake to our students in a world that increasingly urges them to think of their education in instrumental terms, urges them to focus on narrowly defined achievements and material outcomes? [17]

We think a suitable answer starts with a question posed by Leibniz: *"Why are things as they are and not otherwise?"* [18]

Engagement in learning and the joy it can produce starts with asking fundamental questions--the kind of questions children ask as they begin to explore the world. AIS pedagogy is influenced by an educational framework suggested by Alfred North Whitehead. This framework begins with *Romance* ("the subject matter has the vividness of novelty"), followed by *Precision* ("exactness in formulation") and *Generalization* ("a return to romanticism with the added advantage of classified ideas and relevant technique"). Whitehead began and returned to the "romanticism" of asking fundamental questions because he believes *"education must essentially be setting in order of a ferment already stirring in the mind"* [emphasis added].[19]

I sometimes ask myself how it came about that I was the one to develop the theory of relativity. The reason, I think, is that a normal adult never … think[s] about problems of space and time. These are things which he has thought about as a child. But my intellectual development was retarded, as a result of which I began to wonder about space and time only when I had already grown up. [20]

--Albert Einstein

---

17   Faust, Drew, "President Faust, Dean Harris Address Academic Misconduct," *Harvard Magazine,* September-October 2013.

18   Cited in "Leibniz World of Math" at https://mathsimulationtechnology.wordpress.com/ask-why-be-scientist/.

19   Whitehead, Alfred North, *The Aims of Education* (1967), pp. 18-19.

20   Einstein, Albert, cited in Clark, Ronald, *Einstein: The Life and Times* (1971), p. 27.

The "ferment" Whitehead identified is a critical component of *engagement in learning*. It was stated in comparable terms by Augustine when he referred to having a "mind on fire" as he sought to solve the riddle of time.[21] What Whitehead and Augustine describe parallels Mihaly Csikszentmihalyi's conception of flow.[22] Mark Edmundson used the term "absorption" to convey the same feeling:

> Absorption is what occurs when you immerse yourself in something you love. The artist and the poet and the philosopher and the scientist become absorbed . . . . When that happens, time stops and one lives in an ongoing present. One feels whole and at one with oneself. The little boy drawing with his pad on the floor, tongue out from one side of his mouth, is a picture of absorption.[23]

---

21   Augustine, *Confessions* (Chadwick, trans.; 1991), pp. 229, 236. Excerpt:

> This is my reply to anyone who asks: "What was God doing before he made heaven and earth?" My reply is not that which someone is said to have given as a joke to evade the force of the question. He said "He was preparing hells for people who inquire into profundities." It is one thing to laugh, another to see the point at issue, and this reply I reject. I would have preferred him to answer "I am ignorant of what I do not know" rather than reply so as to ridicule someone who asked a deep question . . . .
>
> My mind is on fire to solve this very intricate enigma [of the nature of time]. Do not shut the door, Lord my God. Good Father, through Christ I beg you, do not shut the door to my longing to understand these things . . . . And to whom but you shall I more profitably confess my incompetence? . . . . Grant what I love. For I love, and this love was your gift. Grant it Father . . . . Grant it, since I have undertaken to acquire understanding and "the labour is too much for me" . . . until you open the way. Through Christ I beg you, in the name of him who is the most holy of the holy ones, let no one obstruct my inquiry . . . .

Augustine's mind was "on fire" because he shared a characteristic with thinkers and dedicated researchers in almost every field: a commitment to truth, and a pressing desire that "no one obstruct [his] inquiry" into questions that philosophers, theologians, and scientists have explored throughout history.

22   Csikszentmihalyi, Mihaly. *Flow*, (1990). Excerpt:

> A person can feel pleasure without any effort . . . but it is impossible to enjoy a tennis game, a book, or a conversation, unless attention is fully concentrated on the activity. It is for this reason that pleasure is so evanescent, and that the self does not grow as a consequence of pleasurable experiences. Complexity requires investing psychic energy in goals that are new, that are relatively challenging. It is easy to see this process in children. During the first few years of life every child is a little 'learning machine' trying out new movements, new words daily. The rapt concentration on a child's face as she learns each new skill is a good indication of what enjoyment is about (pp. 46-47).

23   Edmundson, Mark, *The Age of Guilt: The Super-Ego in the Online World* (2023), p. 99.

> *During the first few years of life every child is a little "learning machine" trying out new movements, new words daily. The rapt concentration on a child's face as she learns each new skill is a good indication of what enjoyment is about.* [24]
>
> --Mihaly Csikszentmihalyi

The late E. O. Wilson (Pellegrino University Research Professor at Harvard University and winner of the National Medal of Science) stated a variation of Whitehead's educational framework when he wrote that "[t]he early stages of a creative thought, the ones that count, do not arise from jigsaw puzzles of specialization . . . *the most successful scientist thinks like a poet—wide-ranging, sometimes fantastical—and works like a bookkeeper*" [emphasis added].[25]

Wilson's view that creative thought in the sciences requires a poetic and imaginative sensibility is echoed in an AIS assignment featuring a 1965 Nobel Prize Banquet speech by physicist Richard Feynman. Feynman stated:

> *Imagination* reaches out repeatedly trying to achieve some higher level of understanding, until suddenly I find myself momentarily alone before one new corner of nature's pattern of *beauty* and true *majesty* revealed. That was my reward.
>
> Then, having fashioned tools to make access easier to the new level, I see these tools used by other men straining their imaginations against further *mysteries* beyond. There, are my votes of recognition [emphases added].[26]

---

24   Csikszentmihalyi, (1990), p. 47.

25   Wilson, E. O., *The Meaning of Human Existence* (2014), p. 41.

26   Feynman, Richard, 1965 Nobel Prize Banquet Speech.

Feynman's words (starting with his reference to "imagination") include "beauty," majesty," and "mysteries." This perspective--more often associated with expression in the humanities--captures the joy associated with engagement in learning in any field.

We don't stop playing because we grow old; we grow old because we stop playing. [27]

--George Bernard Shaw

Faculty and staff members who exemplify joy in learning can be found on any college campus. Administrators and student organizations[28] should create more opportunities for them to openly discuss their deepest interests and commitments. Programming examples include "What Matters to Me and Why" forums at Stanford University and University of California-Irvine.[29] A subliminal message conveyed by such forums is that a life immersed in studying, thinking, questioning, and doing is a demonstrable path to fulfillment.

Highly effective teachers ... often discuss openly and enthusiastically their own sense of awe and curiosity about life. [30]

--Ken Bain, *"What the Best College Teachers Do"*

---

27   Shaw, George Bernard, cited in Kaufman, Scott Barry and Gregoire, Carolyn, *Wired to Create: Unraveling the Mysteries of the Creative Mind*, (2016), p. 11.

28   Authors of this book have been active in the support or creation of academic integrity honor codes nationwide. See Pavela, Gary and McCabe, Don "New Honor Codes for a New Generation," *Inside Higher Education*, March, 10, 2005. We think *engagement in learning* and *academic integrity* go hand-in-hand and urge Student Honor Councils or Committees to co-sponsor campus-wide programs like the "What Matters to Me and Why" forums referenced in the text and the note immediately below.

29   See Stanford University and University of California-Irvine "What Matters to me and Why" forum links.

30   Bain, Ken, *What the Best College Teachers Do* (2004) p. 18.

Joy in human connection

One of the most important ethical treatises in history is Aristotle's *Nicomachean Ethics*. About a third of it is devoted to the topic of friendship. Here's a key paragraph we share with AIS students:

> No one would choose to have all good things by himself, for man is a social and political being and his natural condition is to live with others. Consequently a happy man needs society. Since he possesses what is by nature good, it is obviously better for him to spend his days with friends . . . than with any stranger who comes along. It follows that a happy man needs friends.[31]

Jump ahead over 2,000 years and consider this research-based observation from psychiatrist George Vaillant, (Harvard "Grant Study" Director), who said the study team wasn't initially focused on "empathy or attachment," but eventually concluded that "the key to healthy aging is *relationships, relationships, relationships*" [emphasis added].[32]

Antoine de St. Exupery provided a moving insight into the power of relationships when he described the death of his younger brother:

> He was very serious, this younger brother who was about to die in twenty minutes. He had called me in because he felt a pressing need to hand on part of himself to me. "I want to make my will," he said: and he blushed with pride and embarrassment to be talking like a grown man. Had he been the builder of towers he would have bequeathed to me the finishing of his tower. Had he been a father I would have inherited the education of his children. A reconnaissance pilot, he would have passed on to me the intelligence he had gleaned. But he was a child, and what he confided to my care was a toy steam engine, a bicycle, and a rifle.
>
> There is no death when you meet death. When the body sinks into death the essence of man is revealed. Man is a knot, a web, a mesh into which relationships are tied. Only those

---

31   Aristotle, *Nicomachean Ethics*, (1962, Ostwald, trans.), p. 264.

32   Mineo, Liz, "Good Genes are Nice, but Joy is Better." *Harvard Gazette*, April 11, 2017.

relationships matter. The body is an old crock that nobody will miss. I have never known a man to think of himself when dying. Never. [33]

There's nothing new in the suggestion that social connection and co-operation are defining human characteristics and the root of our moral sense. We frequently introduce AIS students to Charles Darwin's observation that "[t]he development of moral qualities [in man] . . . lies in the social instincts [and] the most important elements are love, and the distinct emotion of sympathy." [34]

The healing potential in human relationships is reflected in the ongoing importance of talk therapy in mental health care (often combined with any needed pharmaceuticals). One memorable study in 2001 focused upon the benefits of long term human contact--mainly through the use of four medical follow-up letters a year.[35] The study concluded:

A systematic program of contact with persons who are at risk of suicide and who refuse to remain in the health care system appears to exert a significant preventive influence for at least

---

33   De Saint Exupery, Antoine, *Airman's Odyssey* (2012), p. 387.

34   Darwin, Charles *The Descent of Man,* Norton Critical Edition (2001), pp. 200-201.

35   Motto, Jerome and Bostrom, Alan G., "A Randomized Controlled Trial of Postcrisis Suicide Prevention," *Psychiatric Services* 52(6), June 1, 2001, pp. 828-833

> **ABSTRACT:** This study tested the hypothesis that professionals' maintenance of long-term contact with persons who are at risk of suicide can exert a suicide-prevention influence. This influence was hypothesized to result from the development of a feeling of connectedness and to be most pertinent to high-risk individuals who refuse to remain in the healthcare system.
>
> **METHODS:** A total of 3,005 persons hospitalized because of a depressive or suicidal state, populations known to be at risk of subsequent suicide, were contacted 30 days after discharge about follow-up treatment. A total of 843 patients who had refused ongoing care were randomly divided into two groups; persons in one group were contacted by letter at least four times a year for five years. The other group (the control group) received no further contact. A follow-up procedure identified patients who died during the five-year contact period and during the subsequent ten years. Suicide rates in the contact and no-contact groups were compared.
>
> **RESULTS:** Patients in the contact group had a lower suicide rate in all five years of the study. Formal survival analyses revealed a significantly lower rate in the contact group (p=.04) for the first two years; differences in the rates gradually diminished, and by year 14 no differences between groups were observed.
>
> **CONCLUSIONS:** A systematic program of contact with persons who are at risk of suicide and who refuse to remain in the health care system appears to exert a significant preventive influence for at least two years. Diminution of the frequency of contact and discontinuation of contact appear to reduce and eventually eliminate this preventive influence [emphasis added].

two years. Diminution of the frequency of contact and discontinuation of contact appear to reduce and eventually eliminate this preventive influence.

The authors of the study also referenced a 1989 editorial on suicide prevention by H.G. Moran in the *Journal of the Royal Society of Medicine*:

> [T]here is surely at least one common theme through the centuries--it is the provision of human contact, the comfort of another concerned person, often authoritative but maybe not, conveying a message of hope consonant with the assumptions and values relevant to that particular time. [36]

Supportive relationships between teachers and students are equally important in creating a sense of connection and purpose. Some of the best writing on this topic in recent decades has come from Ken Bain, Ernest Boyer, Carol Dewck, Angela Duckworth, Mark Edmundson, and Parker Palmer, among others. Much of their work is summarized by this observation from Timothy P. Shriver and Jennifer Buffett, authors of the *Handbook of Social Emotional Learning*: "The core of education is the relationship between the teacher and the student, and the extent to which that relationship nurtures the longing of the [student] to matter in the world, and the longing of the teacher to nurture and fulfill that desire."[37]

Building the teacher-student relationship can start with friendly initial encounters, including greeting students by name.[38] Cordiality can then blossom into the impactful relationships described in an 1808

---

36   Morgan, H. G., "Suicide and its Prevention," *Journal of the Royal Society of Medicine* (1989).

37   Shriver, Timothy and Buffet, Jennifer cited in the UC-Berkeley "Greater Good Center" online publication Positive Teacher-Student Relationships (2023). See also the *Handbook of Social and Emotional Learning: Research and Practice* (Shriver and Buffett, 2016).

38   Allday, R. Allan and Pakurar, Kerri, "Effects of Teacher Greetings on Student On-Task Behavior," *Journal of Applied Behavior Analysis* (Summer, 2007). The authors wrote:

> Teachers often report being overwhelmed by the many noninstructional responsibilities of their profession. Furthermore, they frequently balk at implementing complicated and intrusive interventions for individual students . . . . The current research suggests one quick, simple antecedent intervention that can increase student on-task behavior during the first 10 min of class. *Merely greeting a student at the door with his or her name and a brief, genuine pleasantry increased student on-task behavior* [emphasis added].

See also the following observation referenced above in the UC-Berkeley "Greater Good Center" online publication Positive Teacher-Student Relationships:

recollection by Thomas Jefferson about his teachers at the College of William and Mary:

> Under temptations and difficulties I could ask myself what would Dr. Small, Mr. Wythe, Peyton Randolph do in this situation? What course in it will assure me of their approbation? I am certain that this mode of deciding on my conduct tended more to its correctness than any reasoning power I possessed.[39]

Years ago we saw a comparable example of teacher impact in an end-of-year commentary by University of Virginia *Cavalier Daily* staff member (and graduating senior) Katie Dalton. Ms. Dalton wrote about her "best teacher," William Fishback:

> My friendship with you has been the most rewarding relationship to come out of my academic experience. You know just how and when to push me out of procrastination, and you consistently offer support as a father would. More than anyone else, you embody the Jeffersonian ideal of a professor who instructs but also encourages his students, and who values friendships with his pupils as much as their final exams.[40]

The core of education is the relationship between the teacher and the student, and the extent to which that relationship nurtures the longing of the [student] to matter in the world, and the longing of the teacher to nurture and fulfill that desire.

--Timothy Shriver and Jennifer Buffett in the Handbook of Social Emotional Learning.

At the college level, students prefer professors who are approachable—they say "hi" on campus, smile often, and stay after class to talk to students. They also set high expectations, are fair, honest, trustworthy, respectful, open, supportive, and encouraging.

39   Letter from Thomas Jefferson to Thomas Jefferson Randolph, 24 November 1808.

40   Dalton, Katie, University of Virginia *Cavalier Daily* (May 17, 2002).

> *The central qualities that make for successful teaching can be simply stated: command of the material to be taught, a contagious enthusiasm for play of ideas, optimism about human potential, the involvement of one's students, and--not least--sensitivity, integrity, and warmth as a human being. When this combination is present in the classroom, the impact of a teacher can be powerful and enduring.* [41]
>
> --Ernest Boyer, *College: The Undergraduate Experience in America*

No one was better than Leo Tolstoy at describing the joy that can arise from human connection. In *Anna Karenina,* one of his leading characters, Levin, had fallen deeply in love. He took a walk while in that enchanted state and was able to experience the miraculous in everyday life:

> He was moved in particular by two children going to school, some silvery gray pigeons that flew down from the rooftop to the pavement, and some little loaves of bread, sprinkled with flour . . . set out in front of a bakery. . . . [A] little boy ran over to a pigeon, glancing at Levin with a smile; the pigeon flapped its wings and fluttered, gleaming in the sunshine among the snowdust quivering in the air, while the smell of freshly baked bread was wafted out of a little window . . . . All this together was so extraordinarily wonderful that *Levin burst out laughing and crying for joy. . .* [emphasis added].[42]

We probably couldn't endure permanent residence in that world, but neither would we want to miss it entirely. Each variation of human connection described above (friendship, family, therapist-patient, and teacher-student) provides multiple entrances to different attributes of joy.

---

41 Boyer, Ernest, *College: The Undergraduate Experience in America* (1987), p.154.

42 Tolstoy, Leo, *Anna Karenina,* Bantam Classic (2006), p.484

Joy in silence, solitude and reflection

Pico Iyer wrote a memorable description of *creative solitude*: [43]

> We have to earn silence, then, to work for it: to make it not an absence but a presence; not emptiness, but repletion. Silence is something more than just a pause; it is that enchanted place where space is cleared and time is stayed and the horizon itself expands. In silence, we often say, we can hear ourselves think; but what is truer to say is that in silence we can hear ourselves *not think*, and so sink below ourselves into a place far deeper than mere thought allows. [44]

Iyer's description is supported by a growing body of research suggesting that solitude can be used to enhance insight and creativity. [45] Brain scanning in recent years has indicated that different parts of the brain (the inward looking "imagination network" and outward focused executive function) working in tandem can produce a synthesis of creativity and productivity. Scott Barry Kaufman and Carolyn Gregoire, authors of *Wired to Create: Unraveling the Mysteries of the Creative Mind* elaborated on this point in a UC-Berkeley Greater Good Science Center overview of their work:

> Time for solitary reflection truly feeds the creative mind. Neuroscientists have discovered that solitary, inwardly focused reflection employs a different brain network than outwardly focused attention. When our mental focus is directed towards the outside world, the Executive attention network is activated, while the imagination network is typically suppressed. This is why our best ideas don't tend to arise when our attention is fully engaged on the outside world. *It's important to make*

---

43   We define "creative solitude" to mean solitude *chosen* or *managed* to promote personal growth, insight, or service. The word "managed" is necessary to encompass circumstances when individuals subjected to externally imposed solitude turn the experience into wisdom. See, for example, Nelson Mandela, *Long Walk to Freedom: The Autobiography of Nelson Mandela*, 1995.

44   Iyer, Pico, "The Eloquent Sounds of Silence," *Time Magazine*, June 24, 2001

45   See, generally, Storr, Anthony, *Solitude: A Return to Self* (1988) and Kaufman, Scott and Gregoire, Carolyn, *Wired to Create: Unraveling the Mysteries of the Creative Mind* (2016). Additional summaries of research can be found in Jacobs, Tom "Can Solitude Make You More Creative?" UC-Berkeley Greater Good Science Center (January 26, 2018) and https://www.apa.org/monitor/2022/04/cover-science-creativity.

time for solitude, to give yourself space to reflect, make new connections, and find meaning. Unfortunately, solitude is widely undervalued in society, leading many people to shy away from alone time . . . [emphasis added].[46]

Kaufman and Gregoire expanded on the importance of harnessing the executive function to "make time for solitude:"

> Executive control processes support creative thinking by helping us deliberately plan future actions, remember to use various creative tactics . . . [and] keep track of which strategies we've already tried . . . . They also help us *focus* our imagination, blocking out external distractions and allowing us to tune in to our inner experience.[47]

An image of the whole meaning of existence … came to his mind. The image he saw did not seem to be embodied in the work or activity which occupied [him and his companions], which they believed was central to their lives, and by which they were known to others. The meaning of existence was to preserve unspoiled, undisturbed and undistorted the image of eternity with which each person is born. Like a silver moon in a calm, still pond.[48]

--Alexander Solzhenitsyn, *Cancer Ward*

Mental coordination between the executive function and imagination network was anticipated by British psychiatrist Anthony Storr in his book *Solitude*. He concluded that "[t]he happiest lives are probably

---

46   Kaufman, Scott and Gregoire, Carolyn, "Ten Habits of Highly Creative People," UC-Berkeley Greater Good Science Center, January 20, 2016.

47   Kaufman, Scott and Gregoire, Carolyn, *Wired to Create: Unraveling the Mysteries of the Creative Mind* (2016), p. xxviii.

48   Solzhenitsyn, Alexander, *Cancer Ward* (1972), p. 428.

those in which neither interpersonal relationships nor impersonal interests are idealized as the only way to salvation . . . [t]he desire and pursuit of the whole must comprehend both aspects of human nature. . . .[49]

Storr's observation and confirming brain imaging research reiterate the wisdom in Plato's Chariot metaphor. The charioteer must manage different components of the mind to achieve multiple goals, including discovering awe and joy in creative solitude. Helping students understand and initiate this kind of self-management is a key aim in the Academic Integrity Seminar.

How does awe transform us? By quieting the nagging, self-critical, overbearing, status-conscious voice of our self, or ego, and empowering us to collaborate, to open our minds to wonders, and to see the deep patterns of life.[50]

-- Dacher Keltner, Awe: The New Science of Everyday Wonder and How It Can Transform Your Life

---

What happens if the charioteer in Plato's metaphor is overwhelmed? Years ago we saw a relevant student perspective in the Colgate University *Maroon-News* article "Busy Lifestyle Leaves No Room for Philosophical Reflection" by Katherine Wiley. Ms. Wiley wrote:

> At an academic institution, I should be constantly thinking. But I feel so busy here that I don't have time for my thoughts . . . It's not that I'm not thinking. It's just that my thoughts are all about doing. I think and I think and I think, but my thoughts are all concentrated on my actions. My mind has adopted the form of my date book. I am constantly planning what I will do next and when I will be finished so that I can go on to the next necessary activity . . . It's rare that my mind is freed from thoughts like

---

49   Storr, Anthony, *Solitude: A Return to the Self* (2005), Chapter 12. Kindle location 3373.

50   Keltner, Dacher, *Awe: The New Science of Everyday Wonder and How It Can Transform Your Life* (2023), p.xx.

this, giving me the time to really dissect information introduced in class, reading, or by my friends.[51]

Some might say Ms. Wiley was preparing for life in contemporary American society (she'll be fully acclimated when she runs out of time to think about thinking). A better perspective is that her dissatisfaction reveals intuitive insight into needed connections between creative solitude, thoughtful integration of experience, and higher forms of creativity.

A variation of what Ms. Wiley saw at a personal level was described by Saul Bellow as a characteristic of a distracted society--now rendered even more distracted by social media. "I often recall," Bellow wrote,

> . . . a sentence from one of Samuel Butler's essays: "Life is like playing a violin solo in public and learning the instrument as one goes," and then I add that there is a drunken riot in the concert hall, and nobody at all is minding the music . . . . The simile is exaggerated, of course . . . . The grain of truth in it is that when you at last are ready to play, you cannot be sure of your listeners. They will predictably be tormented by a plethora of alternatives. Why should they be here, not elsewhere? And why should they listen to you, not to somebody else? [52]

What assistance can educators offer? One starting point is sharing evocative literature that helps students appreciate the joy associated with awe and the reflective insight.[53] Also, as discussed in Chapter

---

51   Wiley, Katherine, "Busy Lifestyle Leaves No Room for Philosophical Reflection" Colgate University *Maroon-News,* October 1, 1999

52   Bellow, Saul, *It All Adds Up: From the Dim Past to the Uncertain Future* (1995), p.164.

53   AIS Tutors sometimes share this observation by Zen master Thich Nhat Hanh from *Being Peace* (1987, pp. 46-47):

> If you are a poet, you will see clearly that there is a cloud floating in this sheet of paper. Without a cloud there will be no water; without water, the trees cannot grow, and without trees you cannot make paper.

> So the cloud is here . . . . Paper and cloud are so close . . . . And if you look more deeply . . . with the eyes of those who are awake, you see not only the cloud and the sunshine in it, but that everything is here: the

> wheat that became the bread for the logger to eat, the logger's father—everything is in this sheet of paper . . . . The presence of this tiny sheet of paper proves the existence of the whole of the cosmos.

An online version is also available here: https://bit.ly/3YtmHzt.

Two, AIS students are asked to write a gratitude statement modeled on Marcus Aurelius's *Meditations*. This thought exercise--like our "Retirement Banquet" assignment [54]-- is designed to foster personal insight at the deepest level: *Who do I admire? Why are they admirable?* Students are then encouraged to make expressions of gratitude a *habit,* facilitated by Gratitude Journal guidance from the UC-Berkeley Greater Good Science Center. [55]

In the Assignment Five [Gratitude Statement] I was forced to think about the contributions and impacts that my close friends and family have had on me. I've never gone through an exercise like this before. In analyzing what I've learned from each of my family members, I came to a larger understanding of who I was, what is important to me, and how I want to be remembered.

--AIS student comment

Overall, the most important work AIS students are asked to undertake is to make a candid assessment of themselves. How do they want to be perceived later in life? What purposes do they wish to pursue? What qualities of character do they seek in their friends? How can they enhance those qualities in themselves? Are values like trust, reciprocity, responsibility, truth-seeking, and truth-telling ephemeral or foundational

---

54 Academic Integrity Seminar Assignment One:

> Please pretend you're at a retirement banquet. This is a serious and formal occasion, not a "roast." The person retiring is 65 years old and at the end of a long career. You know this person well--both inside and outside the workplace. It's your job to say a few truthful, descriptive words about them. *What character or personality traits come to mind?*

> Question for you to answer: Pretend the person retiring is *you.* In short, we're asking you to project yourself into the future and to identify *at least five* descriptive words you hope others would say about you at a comparable event. By "descriptive words" we mean *single* words or *very short* phrases. Please number each descriptive word or phrase and rank them in priority order (#1 = the most important to you).

> Students are given an optional opportunity at the end of the Seminar to revise their "descriptive words." Most do so, often citing one or more influential Seminar assignments for the change.

55 Greater Good Science Center, UC-Berkeley, gratitude statement guidance and exercise.

for human flourishing? We think insightful answers to all these questions are most likely to occur when students are asked to think about them "deeply and privately," as Mark Edmundson recommends:

If you do not read, deeply and privately, you risk becoming prey to every attractive social consensus that sputters down the highway. You'll become one of those oversocialized beings who cannot step apart and think something through for yourself. [56]

--Mark Edmundson (University Professor of English at the University of Virginia)

Joy in resilience, adaptation, and purpose

How can resilience, adaptation, and purpose be visualized? An AIS assignment described in Chapter Three (Trees of Niu Mountain by Mengzi) is worth repeating here. The poetic scene itself is akin to a solitary visit to a forested mountaintop, but Mengzi also conveys a classic Confucian message (immediately recognized by many international students from China) about the inherent goodness of human nature; how that goodness can be damaged; and how the mind can be trained to replenish it.

Mengzi wrote:

The way in which a man loses his proper goodness of mind is like the way in which the trees are denuded by axes . . . . Cut down day after day, can the mind retain its beauty? But there is a development of its life day and night, and in the calm air of the morning, just between night and day, the mind feels in a degree those desires and aversions which are proper to humanity; but the feeling is not strong, and it is shackled and destroyed by what takes place during the day. This destruction taking place again and again, the restorative influence of

---

56   Edmundson, Mark, *The Age of Guilt* (2023), p. 64.

the night is not sufficient to preserve the proper goodness of the mind. And when this proves insufficient for that purpose, man's nature becomes not much different from that of the irrational animals. When they see this, people think that the mind never had those powers which I assert. But does this condition represent the feelings proper to humanity? [57]

The reading that resonated with me most was the Mengzi reading. Not only did I find his description of human nature beautiful, but I also found it eye opening to the point where I could attach his mindset directly to myself and many people that I know. Before even finishing the assignment, I found myself sharing this insight with my friends.

--AIS student comment

What Mengzi suggested about the potential power of "restorative influences" to overcome loss and anxiety has support in contemporary research. George Vaillant concluded in the Harvard University "Grant Study" of adult development that *"[I]t is not stress that kills us . . . . It is effective adaptation to stress that permits us to live."* [58]

Vaillant later used a supporting metaphor: "[A]n oyster, coping with an irritating grain of sand, creates a pearl . . . . Humans, too, when confronted with irritants, engage in unconscious but often creative behavior." [59]

AIS tutors also highlight Aristotle's guidance on resilience and adaptation:

Now many events happen by chance . . . [some will] turn out ill [and] crush and maim happiness; for they both bring pain with them and hinder many activities. Yet even in these nobility shines

---

57   Mengzi, "The Trees of Niu Mountain" (AIS assignment at https://bit.ly/3FE9hIC).

58   Vaillant, George, *Adaptation to Life* (1977), p. 374.

59   Vaillant, George, *Aging Well*, (2008), Kindle location 1,214.

through, when a man bears with resignation many great misfortunes, not through insensibility to pain but through nobility and greatness of soul . . . . For the man who is truly good and wise, we think, bears all the chances [in] life becomingly *and always makes the best of circumstances, as a good general makes the best military use of the army at his command [even after a defeat] and a good shoemaker makes the best shoes out of the hides that are given him; and so with all other craftsmen . . .*" [emphasis added].[60]

Aristotle isn't associated with the Stoic tradition, but a Stoic perspective is evident in that language--something AIS students also encounter when they read the *Meditations* of Marcus Aurelius.

'It's unfortunate that this has happened.' No. It's fortunate that this has happened and I've remained unharmed by it—not shattered by the present or frightened of the future .... Does what's happened keep you from acting with justice, generosity, self-control, sanity, prudence, honesty, humility, straightforwardness, and all the other qualities that allow a person's nature to fulfill itself? So remember this principle when something threatens to cause you pain: the thing itself was no misfortune at all; to endure it and prevail is great good fortune. [61]

--Marcus Aurelius, *Meditations*

Resilience, adaptation, and purpose featured in AIS "lives of integrity"

The historical figures featured in AIS assignments created purpose-driven lives by developing effective solutions to extraordinary stresses, including intense periods of anxiety and depression. Four related essays in our Appendix elaborate on his theme:

---

60   Aristotle, *Nicomachean Ethics,* Book I (10), (Ross, trans.).

61   Aurelius, Marcus, *Meditations*, Book IV p.48 (Hays, trans.).

- *What Abraham Lincoln Can Teach Contemporary College Students*

- *What Frederick Douglass Can Teach Contemporary College Students*

- *Charles Darwin: A Study in Resilience, Adaptation, and Purpose*

- *Resilience, Adaptation and Purpose: Readings from the Academic Integrity Seminar*

Summary and conclusion

A core insight in Plato's chariot allegory is the difficulty of directing and managing the self to any purpose beyond immediate gratification. Consider this passage in Marcus's *Meditations:*

> Concentrate every minute . . . on doing what's in front of you with precise and genuine seriousness, tenderly, willingly, with justice. And on freeing yourself from all other distractions. Yes, you can—if you do everything as if it were the last thing you were doing in your life, and *stop being aimless, stop letting your emotions override what your mind tells you, stop being hypocritical, self-centered, irritable* [emphasis added]. [62]

Those concluding words don't suggest Marcus had discovered an easy path to fulfillment. He may have defined a purpose, but trying to achieve that purpose was a lifelong task accompanied by multiple failures along the way. Like everyone else, Marcus was struggling with an inherently discordant human nature (including both "noble" and "ignoble" elements). Finding a harmonious balance was hard work.

Understanding Marcus's Stoicism --and his perseverance in practicing it-- requires understanding his belief in a "Universal Nature" or transcendent reason at the heart of the Universe.[63] His belief in this regard

---

62   Aurelius, Marcus, *Meditations. Book II p. 16 (Hays, trans).*

63   Ralph Waldo Emerson provides a comparable perspective in his essay Circles (first series 1841):

> Yet this incessant movement and progression which all things partake could never become sensible to us but by contrast to some principle of fixture or stability in the soul. Whilst the eternal generation of circles proceeds, the eternal generator abides. That central life is somewhat superior to creation, superior to knowledge and thought, and contains all its circles. For ever it labors to create a life and thought as large and excellent as itself; but in vain; for that which is made instructs how to make a better.

enabled him to be "religious" without a personal God and "ethical" without an explicit set of divine commandments. Many Buddhists, Confucianists, and adherents of different schools of Hinduism (among others) share this perspective.

The inevitable question arises in this context whether we can be "good without god." Our qualified answer is "yes," [64] but history suggests that finding some defensible ontological framework may be necessary for most of us. Richard Feynman, for example, was a notable religious skeptic. He asserted a capacity to accept "being lost in the mysterious universe without having any purpose, which is the way it really is as far as I can tell." [65] But even Feynman echoed Marcus Aurelius's transcendent language when he said in his Nobel banquet speech that the pinnacle of his career left him "momentarily alone before one new corner of nature's pattern of beauty and true majesty revealed." [66] Comparable evocative statements from Charles Darwin and Albert Einstein are cited in our introduction. Perhaps scientific work itself doesn't require a religious sensibility, but explaining what the work may mean might.

Every realm of nature is marvelous.... Absence of haphazard and conduciveness of everything to an end are to be found in Nature's works in the highest degree, and the resultant end of her generations and combinations is a form of the beautiful. [67]

--Aristotle

---

64   Albert Camus offered an *unqualified* "yes" to the question "can we be good without god?" The Myth of Sisyphus was his best argument.

65   Feynman, Richard, The Pleasure of Finding Things Out (2005), p. 23.

66   Feynman, Richard, 1965 Nobel Prize Banquet Speech.

67   Aristotle, Parts of Animals, Book I, part 5 (University of Chicago, Ogle trans.).

Seeking to develop a set of feelings and principles regarding the nature of reality and existence--including responsibilities that might be associated with intelligence and sentience--are central to our educational mission. It is for this reason that British mathematician and philosopher Alfred North Whitehead argued in his book *The Aims of Education* that "the essence of education is that it be religious." [68] By "religious" he meant that education should inspire a sense of awe and wonder about the Universe and help us define our responsibilities within it. [69]

> *The essence of education is that it be religious.... A religious education is an education which inculcates duty and reverence. Duty arises from our potential control over the course of events. Where attainable knowledge could have changed the issue, ignorance has the guilt of vice. And the foundation of reverence is this perception, that the present holds within itself the complete sum of existence, backwards and forwards, that whole amplitude of time, which is eternity.*
>
> -- Alfred North Whitehead

Contemporary secular universities often avoid words like "duty," "reverence," or any ontological perspectives at all. "Academic integrity," for example, is typically described as an unexplained end in itself, or a set of utilitarian policies designed to preserve academic quality and reputation. "Integrity" of the *individual soul or character* grounded on

---

68   Whitehead, Alfred North, *The Aims of Education* (1967), p. 14.

69   A similar perspective was stated by the eminent microbiologist Rene Dubos in A God Within (1972) p. 255:

> Religion and science also constitute deep-rooted and ancient efforts to find richer experience and deeper meaning than are found in the ordinary biological and social satisfactions. . . Both the myths of religion and the laws of science . . . [are] symbolic expressions of cosmic truths. Those truths may always remain beyond human understanding, but at every stage of human development glimpses of them have enriched man in experience and comprehension. Together, religion and science make human life more than a flash of occasional enjoyments lighting up a mass of pain and misery. They . . . convert it into an adventure of the spirit.

truth-seeking and truth-telling [70] is, at best, a historical vestige kept in deep background.

Many suggestions in this book highlight alternative approaches to student development, focused on *mentoring, teaching*, and *campus programming*. In terms of mentoring at the deepest level, a magnificent role model is the late Philip Rhinelander, a professor of humanities emeritus and Dean of Humanities and Sciences at Stanford University. James Stockdale, author of *Courage Under Fire: Testing Epictetus's Doctrines in a Laboratory of Human Behavior* took classes at Stanford while he was a naval officer and subsequently described his encounter with Rhinelander:

> A voice boomed out of an office, "Can I help you?" The speaker was Philip Rhinelander, dean of Humanities and Sciences, who taught 'Philosophy 6: The Problems of Good and Evil.' At first he thought I was a professor, but we soon found common ground in the Navy because he'd served in World War II. Within fifteen minutes we'd agreed that I would enter his two-term course in the middle, and to make up for my lack of background, I would meet him for an hour a week for a private tutorial in the study of his campus home . . . . On my last session, he reached high in his wall of books and brought down a copy of *The Enchiridion* [by the Stoic philosopher Epictetus]. He said, "I think you'll be interested in this." [71]

We know, of course, that Stockdale's subsequent "interest" in Epictetus sustained him and many of his colleagues during years of harsh treatment as a prisoner of war.

The kind of effective teaching we have in mind is also exemplified by an ongoing course at Harvard University, described in a 2013 *Atlantic* article by Christine Gross-Loh, Why Are Hundreds of Harvard Students Studying Ancient Chinese Philosophy? Gross-Loh wrote that "[Michael]

---

70   One way to explore an orientation toward truth-seeking and truth-telling with students is to introduce them to this observation from Charles Darwin (also referenced in Chapter Three):

> I believe there exists, & I feel within me, an instinct for truth, or knowledge or discovery, of something same nature as the instinct of virtue, & that our having such an instinct is reason enough for scientific researches without any practical results ever ensuing from them

71   Stockdale, James, (1993), pp. 1-2.

Puett's course Classical Chinese Ethical and Political Theory has become the third most popular course at the university . . . The only classes with higher enrollment are Intro to Economics and Intro to Computer Science . . . ." She concluded that one reason for the appeal of Puett's course was that "students are also lured in by Puett's bold promise: *This course will change your life*" [emphasis added]. [72]

Michael Puett's academic biography is described at a Harvard website. He is now the "Walter C. Klein Professor of Chinese History and Anthropology" at the University and a recipient of "the Joseph R. Levenson Memorial Teaching Prize, the Everett Mendelsohn Excellence in Graduate Mentoring Award, the Star Family Prize for Excellence in Advising, and the Harvard College Professorship for Excellence in Undergraduate Teaching." We cite some of Puett's awards in support of the idea that American higher education can still encourage teaching designed to appeal to the heart and spirit. Mark Edmundson, University Professor at the University of Virginia (repeatedly cited in our book) also exemplifies this characteristic. [73]

Puett and co-author Christine Gross-Loh wrote a book about his Harvard Course titled *The Path*. The book includes a chapter focused on the work of Mencius (or Mengzi), a thinker featured in AIS assignments for over 15 years. Mencius is associated with the view that human nature is grounded on goodness (sociability) and that people can best manage a chaotic world by strengthening and habituating that capacity.

Puett explained how Mencius can be both deeply insightful and accessible to students at the same time:

> Mencius is no serene Buddha, no selfless Jesus. Far from being a placid and benign wise man, he comes across as a brilliant, mercurial, strong-willed, arrogant, and complicated figure—a man who struggled to achieve goodness and at times failed to live up to his own philosophy. [74]

---

72   Gross-Loh, Christine Why Are Hundreds of Harvard Students Studying Ancient Chinese Philosophy?, *The Atlantic, April 8, 2013.*

73   See, especially, Edmundson, Mark, The Heart of the Humanities: Reading, Writing, Teaching (2018).

74   Puett, Michael and Gross-Loh, Christine Gross-Loh *The Path* (2016), p. 61.

Based on that description, students can see that Plato's chariot allegory fits Mencius as well as any other historical figure we describe.

> *I really appreciated the Mengzi assignment.... I started researching more of his work after completing that assignment and I was able to draw life lessons that can apply to different areas of my life ... I am grateful for this seminar experience. It's going to help guide my moral compass moving forward, and I can't wait to see the positive effects that it will have on my life.*
>
> *--AIS Student comment*

Campus programming --especially the choice of commencement and convocation speakers--can also help create opportunities to reflect upon a broader sense of meaning. Among many suitable examples, speakers like Alexander Solzhentsyn, Martha Nussbaum and Vaclav Havel have introduced students to foundational insights rarely heard in contemporary classrooms:

Alexander Solzhentsyn 1978 Harvard commencement speech:

If humanism were right in declaring that man is born only to be happy, he would not be born to die. Since his body is doomed to die, his task on earth evidently must be of a more spiritual nature. It cannot be unrestrained enjoyment of everyday life. It cannot be the search for the best ways to obtain material goods and then cheerfully get the most of them. It has to be the fulfillment of a permanent, earnest duty so that one's life journey may become an experience of moral growth, so that one may leave life a better human being than one started it. [75]

---

75   Solzhenitsyn, Alexander, 1978 Harvard commencement speech. Available at "NPR: The Best Commencement Speeches ever." **Verified transcript at the** American Rhetoric Online Speech Bank.

Martha Nussbaum 2003 at Georgetown University:

World citizenship is impossible when the powerful define their humanity in terms of possessions, rather than the goods of the soul. As the Greek philosophers long ago remarked, the goods of the soul are such that we can all strive toward them harmoniously: one person's attainment of them reinforces, and does not undermine another's. Material goods, by contrast, always cause conflict, especially when the goal is limitless accumulation, not merely sustenance. So world citizenship, and the compassion that supports it, must be built on the goods of the soul. [76]

Vaclav Havel 2011 at Independence Hall:

Transcendence as a hand reached out to those close to us, to foreigners, to the human community, to all living creatures, to nature, to the Universe; transcendence as a deeply and joyously experienced need to be in harmony even with what we ourselves are not, what we do not understand, what seems distant from us in time and space, but with which we are nevertheless mysteriously linked because, together with us, all this constitutes a single world. Transcendence as the only real alternative to extinction. [77]

Teachers and staff members on your campus could address and personalize comparable perspectives. As previously suggested, one proven way of doing so is through "What Matters to Me and Why" forums, sponsored by different academic departments or organizations like a Student Honor Council.

---

76   Nussbaum, Martha. 2003 Georgetown University commencement speech. Available at Humanity: Commencement Speech Archive (#5).

77   Havel, Vaclav, 2011 address at Independence Hall. Havel offered a similar perspective in his 1995 Harvard Commencement Speech:

> Naturally, I am not suggesting that modern people be compelled to worship ancient deities and accept rituals they have long since abandoned. I am suggesting something quite different: we must come to understand the deep mutual connection or kinship between the various forms of our spirituality. We must recollect our original spiritual and moral substance, which grew out of the same essential experience of humanity. I believe that this is the only way to achieve a genuine renewal of our sense of responsibility for ourselves and for the world. And at the same time, it is the only way to achieve a deeper understanding among cultures that will enable them to work together in a truly ecumenical way to create a new order for the world.

Universities can play a critical role in expanding student horizons and reducing destructive divisions in our society.[78] Doing so will entail remaining open to a broader sense of meaning, including a commitment to *truth-seeking and truth-telling* implicit in our academic integrity programming. The Academic Integrity Seminar was designed with those aims in mind.

A concluding suggestion from the authors: This book has been influenced by insights shared with us by college administrators, students, and teachers nationwide. We are grateful for their assistance. Please continue the discussion on our Academic Integrity Facebook Group (over 1,100 colleagues and growing). Updates to our book will appear there.

---

[78] Some commentators suggest universities have played a substantial role in *creating* the current cultural divide. See Haidt, Jonathan, "Academia and the Anxious Generation: How Universities Lost the Trust of America" video available at Real Clear Politics (February 9, 2024) and Zakaria, Fareed "Why University Presidents Are Under Fire" CNN December 10, 2023. Zakaria wrote:

> As CNN's Van Jones has eloquently said, the point of college is to keep you physically safe but intellectually unsafe, to force you to confront ideas that you disagree with passionately . . . . What we saw in the House hearing this week was the inevitable result of decades of the politicization of universities. America's top colleges are no longer seen as bastions of excellence but as partisan outfits, which means they will keep getting buffeted by these political storms as they emerge. They should abandon this long misadventure into politics, retrain their gaze on their core strengths and rebuild their reputations as centers of research and learning.

Introduction to Seminar Content: *What Abraham Lincoln Can Teach Contemporary Students*

By Gary Pavela

(Adapted from a speech sponsored by the U.S. Department of Education and delivered to Virginia Tech University faculty and staff after the April 16, 2007 rampage shooting).

Preliminary note: *One of the most popular assigned readings in the* Academic Integrity Seminar *is Joshua Wolf Shenk's* "Lincoln's Great Depression." *We chose this reading, in part, because we believe ethical development is most likely to occur through direct observation of admirable lives. Lincoln's example serves that purpose in multiple ways, including his love of learning, skillful adaptation to loss and failure, and his determination to define and pursue a cause greater than himself. Lincoln is fascinating to contemporary college students because he exemplifies an almost unimaginable possibility: personal happiness (as typically defined) may be less important than worthy accomplishment.*

Please consider the following profile of a troubled young adult, based on an actual case history:

- Talked about suicide for weeks at a time.

- Reportedly wrote poetry about thrusting a dagger in his heart and "draw[ing] blood in showers!"

- Was known to "go crazy," requiring the removal of knives and dangerous items from his room.

- Wandered around with a gun during periods of suicidal ideation.

- Collapsed while speaking openly of his hopelessness and thoughts of suicide.

- Was eventually diagnosed with "recurrent major depression."

Who was this risk to himself and to society?

The answer is Abraham Lincoln. My primary sources are Joshua Wolf Shenk's award winning book *Lincoln's Melancholy: How Depression Challenged a President and Fueled His Greatness* (2006) and, secondarily, the analysis of William Lee Miller, author of *Lincoln's Virtues*, (2002); Doris Kearns Goodwin, author of *Team of Rivals: The Political Genius of Abraham Lincoln* (2006) and Carl Sandburg, *The Prairie Years and The War Years*, V.3 (1960).

Lincoln's iconic status can be an impediment to educators. Students are rightly skeptical about what they can learn from god-like figures immortalized in granite. Recent scholarship, however, has opened a new window on Lincoln as a person--his emotional intelligence, and his adaptive skills in coping with adversity, failure, loss, and depression. These are precisely the qualities that need emphasis in the present generation. They're also qualities best understood in the context of a life story, even if the surface of the story is as well known as that of Abraham Lincoln.

There's little doubt Lincoln faced a recurring battle with something akin to clinical depression. A letter he wrote in 1841 reveals the depth of the condition [emphasis added]:

> For not giving you a general summary of news, you must pardon me; it is not in my power to do so. I am now the most miserable man living. *If what I feel were equally distributed to the whole human family, there would not be one cheerful face on the earth.* Whether I shall ever be better I can not tell; I awfully

forebode I shall not. To remain as I am is impossible; I must die or be better, it appears to me. The matter you speak of on my account, you may attend to as you say, unless you shall hear of my condition forbidding it. I say this, because I fear I shall be unable to attend to any bussiness [sic] here, and a change of scene might help me. If I could be myself, I would rather remain at home with Judge Logan. I can write no more. Your friend, as ever, --A. LINCOLN

A fellow legislator in Illinois (Robert L. Wilson) saw the extent of Lincoln's "melancholy" in 1836:

> In a conversation with him about that time (1836), he told me that although he appeared to enjoy life rapturously, still he was the victim of terrible melancholy. He sought company, and indulged in fun and hilarity without restraint, or stint as to time. Still when by himself, he told me that he was so overcome with mental depression, that he never dare carry a knife in his pocket. As long as I was intimately acquainted with him, previous to the commencement of the practice of the law, he never carried a pocket knife, still he was not a misanthropic. He was kind and tender in his treatment to others.

Colleges are attracting more students with disabilities, including students with mood disorders. Those students have much to gain by studying the adaptive strategies of a person who turned his "melancholy" into a source of strength and wisdom for himself and the nation.

How did Lincoln do it?

[1] Learning from suffering.

Lincoln had the courage to go to the core of his suffering and seek a solution. That solution entailed defining and pursuing a high calling. Shenk and biographer Ward H. Lamon cite the following statement Lincoln reportedly made to his friend Joshua Speed (the quotation is from Lamon's *Life of Abraham Lincoln*):

> [H]e told Speed, referring probably to his inclination to commit suicide, "that he had done nothing to make any human being remember that he had lived, and to connect his name with the events transpiring in his day and generation and so impress himself upon them as to link his name with something that would redound to the interest of his fellow man was what he desired to life for." [H]e [later] reminded Speed [of this conversation] at the time. . . he issued the Emancipation Proclamation.

It may not be possible or desirable to root out the sometimes problematical inclination to "link [our] names" with something important (an impulse turned to destructive ends in the school shooting phenomenon). It remains in everyone's interest, however, to help young people understand that lasting respect comes not out of adolescent images of power, but the accomplishment of something that "redound[s] to the interest of [their] fellow man." Harvard University psychiatrist George Vaillant made a similar point when he wrote that the therapist's (and educator's) goal is not to find and advance perfect specimens (if such beings exist), but to "help the paranoid's projection become a novel, an eccentric's sexual fantasy become a sculpture, and a delinquent's impulse to murder evolve into creative lawmaking . . . ." (*Adaptation to Life*, 1977, p. 374).

[2] Defining a goal.

Deciding to pursue a "high calling" requires particularity. What, precisely, is the aim? The answer in Lincoln's case was the fundamental principle of human equality set forth in the Declaration of Independence. This is what he said in a February 22, 1861 speech in Independence Hall, Philadelphia:

> [A]ll the political sentiments I entertain have been drawn, so far as I have been able to draw them, from the sentiments which originated, and were given to the world from this hall in which we stand. I have never had a feeling politically that did not spring from the sentiments embodied in the Declaration of Independence . . . . It was not the mere matter of the separation

of the colonies from the mother land; but something in that Declaration giving liberty, not alone to the people of this country, but hope to the world for all future time.

The danger of not defining fundamental goals is captured by the expression: "having lost sight of our objective we redoubled our efforts." One of the primary aims of a liberal education is to help students define objectives--if only as working hypotheses--that will inspire commitment to a cause greater than themselves. It is when they "forget themselves" in such a cause that the destructive pain of self-absorption subsides.

[3] Thinking about thinking.

Joshua Wolf Shenk discussed Lincoln's reference in the First Inaugural Address to "the better angels of our nature." Those words came from a man who appreciated the competing and contradictory claims of the human psyche. But there are other examples in Lincoln's political writing reflecting the insight that learning how to think could be essential to survival. In an 1862 message to Congress Lincoln wrote that:

> The dogmas of the quiet past, are inadequate to the stormy present. The occasion is piled high with difficulty, and we must rise -- with the occasion. As our case is new, so we must think anew, and act anew. We must disenthrall ourselves, and then we shall save our country.

What Lincoln saw as essential to national survival was also a quality he used to save himself. Psychologists and psychiatrists refer in this regard to the strengthening of a "higher" or "observer" self, able to step back from and evaluate the immediate flow of emotion. It's a quality captured in a December 1974 interview by Sam Keen with Italian psychiatrist Roberto Assagioli:

> I believe the will is the Cinderella of modern psychology, It has been relegated to the kitchen. The Victorian notion that will power could overcome all obstacles was destroyed by Freud's discovery of unconscious motivation. But, unfortunately, this led modern psychology into a deterministic view of man as a

bundle of competing forces with no centre. This is contrary to every human being's direct experience of himself. At some point, perhaps in a crisis when danger threatens, an awakening occurs in which the individual discovers his will . . . . With the certainty that one has a will comes the realization of the intimate connection between the will and the self . . . . It is self-consciousness that sets man apart from animals. Human beings are aware but also know that they are aware.

This insight led to Assagioli's aphorism: *"I have emotions, but I am not my emotions."*

We published a case study of a college student suicide (drawing upon notebook marginalia the victim left behind) in our book *Questions and Answers on College Student Suicide* (2006). The student showed evidence he was beginning to use, but had not yet developed the potential of the "observer self:"

> Can I ever teach? Will I ever cure stuttering? Job interviews, phone calls. People notice *or am I blowing this out of proportion?* [emphasis supplied]

It's commonplace in higher education to speak of teaching students "how to think." This is not an aim to be attempted lightly. It should be one of our highest priorities--a phenomenon that must be continuously studied, evaluated, and revitalized. The goal goes beyond career preparation. For human beings, thinking about thinking is necessary to life itself.

[4] Nurturing a love of learning.

People who knew Lincoln well referred to him as a "stubborn reader." William Lee Miller provides this description:

> It would be quite a study to go through the available record to identify all the places, times, and postures in which those who had known Lincoln in Indiana and in New Salem remembered him reading a book: reading while the horse rests at the end of

a row, reading while walking down the street, reading under a tree, reading while others went to dances, reading with his legs up as high as his head, reading between customers in the post office, reading snatched at length on the counter of the store.

There may be many reasons why Lincoln loved reading. For all his outward gregariousness he was a solitary man, rarely revealing himself to others. Reading was an antidote to loneliness and a way for a precocious mind to find companionship. Lincoln's love of reading also had much to do with a drive for self-improvement--especially after he had defined a higher goal for his life.

Troubled college students sometimes make the mistake of regarding reading and studying as stressful diversions from their inner turmoil. The opposite is true. Few pursuits are more conducive to mental health than engagement in learning. A mind turned inward on itself is wandering in barren terrain.

Students might also be introduced to the idea that engagement in learning is conducive to success in a career. Lincoln demonstrated this prospect in multiple ways, typified by his ability to turn a fascination with Euclidean geometry into legal and political insight. The authors at Math Open Reference wrote that "Abraham Lincoln studied Euclid for training in reasoning, and as a traveling lawyer on horseback, kept a copy of Euclid's Elements in his saddlebag." Lincoln later observed:

> In the course of my law reading I constantly came upon the word "demonstrate." I thought at first that I understood its meaning, but soon became satisfied that I did not. I said to myself, What do I do when I demonstrate more than when I reason or prove? How does demonstration differ from any other proof?
>
> I consulted Webster's Dictionary. They told of "certain proof," "proof beyond the possibility of doubt;" but I could form no idea of what sort of proof that was. I thought a great many things were proved beyond the possibility of doubt, without recourse to any such extraordinary process of reasoning as I

understood demonstration to be. I consulted all the dictionaries and books of reference I could find, but with no better results. You might as well have defined blue to a blind man.

At last I said,-- Lincoln, you never can make a lawyer if you do not understand what *demonstrate* means; and I left my situation in Springfield, went home to my father's house, and stayed there till I could give any proposition in the six books of Euclid at sight. I then found out what demonstrate means, and went back to my law studies.

Math Open Reference concluded that "Lincoln's logical speeches and some of his phrases such as 'dedicated to the proposition' in the Gettysburg address are attributed to his reading of Euclid."

[5] Blending friendship, solitude, and empathy.

Joshua Wolf Shenk cited a letter Lincoln wrote to his best friend Joshua Speed in 1842, shortly after Speed was married. Lincoln was 33 years old at the time:

> How miserably things seem to be arranged in this world. If we have no friends, we have no pleasure, and if we have them we are sure to lose them, and be doubly pained by the loss . . . . I feel somewhat jealous of both of you now [Speed and his wife]; you will be so exclusively concerned with one another, that I shall be forgotten entirely.

Reading that needy letter and visiting the Lincoln Memorial is a disconcerting experience. Lincoln as a human being and Lincoln portrayed in a monument (modeled on the Temple of Zeus in Olympia, Greece) evoke two distinctly different feelings. The former better suits our educational aims.

Lincoln's bond with Joshua Speed was exceptional. The depth of the relationship may be associated with Lincoln's need for companionship during a time of personal doubt and turmoil. But, as suggested earlier, Lincoln also found solace in solitude, especially as he grew older. Shenk wrote:

> Lincoln did little to cultivate intimacy with his wife, or with any other person. His colleagues on the [law] circuit, though they liked and admired him, also felt an impassable distance from him. The one relationship that had obviously transcended business, with Joshua Speed, was by the late 1840s clearly a thing of the past.

Why did the relationship with Speed wane? One answer--suggested by Shenk and other scholars--is that Speed eventually became a slaveholder. As much as Lincoln valued Speed's friendship, he valued the sentiments in the Declaration of Independence more.

One quality in Lincoln that never seemed to diminish was a capacity for empathy. It was evident in his youth (evidenced by multiple stories of his rescuing animals in distress) and could be seen in his conscious effort to understand the perspectives of those which whom he disagreed.

The capacity for empathy also helped Lincoln moderate his own faults. Kearns wrote:

> To be sure, there were times when Lincoln lost his temper, but then he would promptly follow up with a kind gesture. "I was a little cross," he wrote one of his generals, "I ask pardon. If I do get up a little temper I have no sufficient time to keep it up." By such gestures, repeated again and again, he repaired injured feelings that might have escalated into lasting animosity.

What insights can we explore with students about these complex characteristics in Lincoln's life? One answer is that simplistic bromides in self-help manuals fail to capture the complexity of the human heart. Love and friendship are essential to happiness (as Lincoln felt intensely), but exhorting someone with Lincoln's personality to turn away from solitude would be to try to divert him from a central source of comfort and strength. Lincoln balanced his capacity for friendship with deep intellectual interests and overriding social commitments. All three gave meaning to his life. Finding that balance was probably easier because Lincoln could also feel and express love through the quality of empathy, generously shared.

[6] Maintaining humility in the face of mystery.
No one can begin to learn from Lincoln's life and personality without understanding his humility about ultimate knowledge. At a more superficial level, in terms of recognizing his own intellectual powers, Lincoln was far from humble. In this context his "rail splitter" image has the feel of being an artifice--an amusing deception he probably enjoyed. But on deeper matters of religion and faith he genuinely seemed to suspend judgment. Man could not know. And for all man does know every event in life was determined long ago. An approving crowd may have admired the religious tone in Lincoln's Second Inaugural Address, but it was religion of a different sort than many of them heard in church:

> Each [side in the war] looked for an easier triumph, and a result less fundamental and astounding. Both read the same Bible and pray to the same God, and each invokes His aid against the other. It may seem strange that any men should dare to ask a just God's assistance in wringing their bread from the sweat of other men's faces, but let us judge not, that we be not judged. The prayers of both could not be answered. That of neither has been answered fully. *The Almighty has His own purposes* (emphasis supplied).

Lincoln's God was distant and impenetrable. Yet each person remains morally responsible. At one level this perspective is confusing and frightening. At another it's reassuring. We have a duty to do our best. Peace comes with the lucid awareness that any final judgment about whether we have failed our succeeded will be made by a power greater than our own. The universe is not ours to manage--and we should be eternally thankful it isn't.

[7] Refocusing the mind: the role of work and humor.
A consistent theme in Lincoln's life is his deliberate management of mental focus. This is a form of cognitive therapy before the term was invented. Shenk and biographer Ward H. Lamon cited an example in an 1842 letter from Lincoln to Speed:

> I think if I were you, in case my mind were not exactly right, I would avoid being idle. I would immediately engage in some business, or go to making preparations for it.

More useful practical advice would be hard to find. Again, the fundamental understanding is that the mind turned "outward" to worthy pursuits is likely to shape a more desirable, bearable, and sustainable interior landscape.

Lincoln also used humor as a diversion. Carl Sandburg quoted one contemporary observer who didn't understand this dynamic (and who must have been blind to the melancholy on Lincoln's face) as saying "[c]an this man Lincoln ever be serious?"

There were times when Lincoln's humor was simply good-natured fun. Sandburg told the story of "[a] newly elected Congressman [who] came in, [and] Lincoln knowing him to have a sense of humor, [said] 'Come in here and tell me what you know. It won't take long.'" But Sandburg and most other Lincoln scholars also saw Lincoln's humor as a practiced form of diversion. This example from Sandburg highlights that point:

> On the day after [the lost battle at] Fredericksburg the staunch old friend, Issac N. Arnold, entered Lincoln's office and was asked to sit down. Lincoln then read [a joke from a book by the humorist] Artemus Ward . . . . That Lincoln should wish to read this nonsense while the ambulances were yet hauling thousands of wounded from the frozen mud flats of the Rappahannock River was amazing to Congressman Arnold. As he said afterward he was "shocked." He inquired, "Mr. President, is it possible that with the whole land bowed in sorrow and covered with a pall in the presence of yesterday's fearful reverse, you can indulge in such levity?" Then, Arnold said, the President threw down the Artemus Ward book, tears streamed down his cheeks, his physical frame quivered as he burst forth, "Mr. Arnold, if I could not get momentary respite from the crushing burden I am constantly carrying, my heart would break!" And with that pent-up cry let out, it came over Arnold that the laughter of Lincoln at times was a mask.

[8] Learning from failure.

Widespread in popular literature is the "Lincoln's Failures" list. One version includes the following examples (with one notable success at the end):

- 1832 defeated for state legislature

- 1833 failed in business

- 1836 nervous breakdown

- 1843 defeated for nomination to Congress

- 1849 rejected for land officer

- 1854 defeated for U.S. Senate

- 1856 defeated in run for nomination for Vice-President

- 1858 defeated for Senate again

- 1860 elected President of the United States

These lists are deficient because they fail to mention corresponding successes. Nonetheless, any two or three such failures might be sufficient to derail a career or a life. Lincoln persisted. He persisted, in part, because he defined a higher goal beyond his own success or failure. With that goal in mind he became a practitioner of "wise failure." Each defeat, properly understood, provided knowledge and experience for subsequent success.

Contemporary students often lack skills in adapting to and learning from failure. For some the first B- in college represents the end of all hope. How can educators help? The best place to start is with candid discussion of our personal experiences in learning how to fail wisely. Ken Bain makes this point in his book *What the Best College Teachers Do* (2004):

> Highly effective teachers tend to reflect a strong trust in students . . . . They often display openness with students and may, from time to time, talk about their own intellectual journey, its ambitions, triumphs, frustrations, and failures, and encourage

their students to be similarly reflective and candid. They may discuss how they developed their interests, the major obstacles they faced in mastering the subject, or some of their secrets for learning particular material. They often discuss openly and enthusiastically their own sense of awe and curiosity about life. *Above all, they tend to treat students with what can only be called simple decency* (emphasis supplied).

We learn better from example than by precept. For many students, Lincoln's skillful adaptations to a mental disorder are hiding in plain sight. Educators can bring those skills alive by discussion, elaboration, and reiteration, or simply by joining students in reading a suitable book (e.g. Shenk's *Lincoln's Melancholy*). Doing so would also convey an important underlying message: Students with mental disorders can be part of the creative diversity colleges seek to promote.

Friendship Fidelity and Academic Integrity

What follows is the revised text of a speech given by Gary Pavela on August 23, 2004 to the incoming class at Trinity University in San Antonio, Texas. It incorporates many themes in the Academic Integrity Seminar.

The occasion for the speech was the inauguration of Trinity's new academic honor code--the result of a five year effort by students, administrators, and faculty members. The theme of the speech is that values associated with worthy friendships correspond with values that support academic integrity.

Although the speech was given before an audience of several hundred students, it contains questions designed to encourage active participation.

Academic integrity and social trust (a glance at the ceiling)

This is a beautiful auditorium, and I'm especially impressed with the ceiling. Please take a moment and look up at it. Consider the fact that many tons of steel and concrete are perched precariously above your head--probably put up there by the lowest bidder.

My point is that all of us, at this precise moment, depend upon the honesty and integrity of the people who designed and built the building. Multiply this example by countless others and you'll understand the imperative of social trust. We're not talking about an obscure or unimportant topic.

One of the reasons why colleges and universities pay so much attention to academic integrity is the critical need for social trust. Trinity is one of the best small universities in the country. It's preparing you for positions of leadership in the larger society. So the academic integrity standards set by the University (and your fellow students on the new Honor Council) will be demanding.

Is business ethics a contradiction in terms?

How many of you expect to work in business after you graduate? [about one-third of the audience raised their hand]. How many of you think the term "business ethics" is a contradiction in terms? [a scattering of hands were raised]. Federal Reserve Board Chairman Alan Greenspan doesn't share that view. In a 1999 commencement speech at Harvard University he said that:

> Beyond [a] personal sense of satisfaction, having a reputation for fair dealing is a profoundly practical virtue. We call it "good will" in business and add it to our balance sheets. Trust is at the root of any economic system based on mutually beneficial exchange. In virtually all transactions, we rely on the word of those with whom we do business. Were this not the case, exchange of goods and services could not take place on any reasonable scale. Our commercial codes and contract law presume that only a tiny fraction of contracts, at most, need be adjudicated. If a significant number of businesspeople violated the trust upon which our interactions are based, our court system and our economy would be swamped into immobility.

As social trust declines, information-based economies decline with it--and very quickly.

Building the structure of the self

But there's another reason why colleges and universities pay so much attention to academic integrity, beyond the practical imperative of preserving social trust. In addition to the physical structures around us, there's something else that requires integrity to build well: *The structure of the self.*

In one of my previous jobs, a long time ago, I read arguments and counter-arguments made in federal criminal white collar crime cases--appeals of felony convictions. It's striking how the personalities of the defendants in those cases converge with personalities of students I've met who engaged in repeated acts of academic dishonesty. They all seem to share three perspectives:

- "It's a dog-eat-dog world" (competitiveness and gamesmenship are everything).

- "I am (or will be) the top dog, since I'm smarter than everybody else."

- "Friends may be useful in helping me stay or become top dog, but they're otherwise dispensable." (Most cheaters know they're gaining an unfair advantage over other students, just like dishonest corporate executives know they're defrauding their colleagues and co-workers).

How are most white collar criminals convicted? The answer is that most convictions occur because "dispensable" friends of the defendant (who knew all along they were dispensable) enter into plea agreements and testify for the government. Read relevant news stories and see how often that happens.

It's depressing to see the result of these cases. The lives wasted. The human potential lost. But you can see something similar without going into a courtroom. It can be found in the bleakness and sense of emptiness associated with the exclusive view of life as a contest or game, where the goal is to be top dog--a winner above all else, before anyone else. A researcher named Michael Maccoby studied this way of looking at life and wrote about his findings in a book called *The Gamesman*. What happens to a Gamesman late in life? Maccoby wrote:

> An old and tiring gamesman is a pathetic figure, especially after he has lost a few contests, and with them, his confidence. Once his youth, vigor, and even the thrill of winning are lost, he becomes depressed and goalless, questioning the purpose of his life. No longer energized by the . . . struggle and unable to dedicate himself to something he believes in beyond himself . . . he finds himself starkly alone. His attitude has kept him

from deep friendship and intimacy. Nor has he sufficiently developed abilities that would strengthen the self, so that he might gain satisfaction from understanding (science) or creating (invention, art).

Think back for a moment to the betrayal of friendship (superficial, dispensable friendship) in the white collar crime cases. There are contrary examples. In wartime, for example, men and women have died for their friends--willingly sacrificed their lives for their friends. In those instances, however, the friends did not see each other primarily in terms of personal ambition. They shared *fidelity* to each other on deeper grounds, as part of a community, a unit (a band of brothers), or a family.

Please keep the word fidelity in mind. It has two compatible meanings:

- Fidelity to a friend means being true to the friendship.

- And fidelity also means conformity to truth itself.

Let's explore this idea further.

The role of truth and friendship in forming a self

Please think of your best friend. What key words describe the qualities of your friend's character? Let's pause for a moment. Let those words come to your mind.

- How many of you used the word "loyal," or something similar? [nearly everyone in the audience raised their hand].

- How many of you used the word "Honest" or something similar? [nearly everyone in the audience raised their hand].

- How many used "crafty and deceitful" or something similar? [laughter, and one hand raised].

- You see again the rich meaning of the word *fidelity*. A friend is someone loyal to us, but also honest and loyal to the truth.

Let me ask another question. How many of you have found yourself adopting the mannerism of a friend or family member? A certain expression? A way of laughing? [nearly everyone in the audience raised their hand]. What if our self (or a good part of it) is a blend of the key people in our lives? Maybe we know that's true, and seek friendship because doing so has something to do with creating a self. The implications are obvious: Choose your friends carefully. At the physical level, we are what we eat. At the spiritual level--the level of the higher self--we are who we love.

The professional friend exercise

Let's pursue this topic just a bit further. Please pretend your parents decided you needed a professional friend, so they paid someone (secretly) $500 a month to be your friend. You don't know about this, of course. The instructions your parents gave to your professional friend were to build your self-esteem. By that they mean:

- Always to flatter you

- Always to praise you

- Never to criticize you

- And never, ever, be a burden on you by asking you for help.

My hunch is that most of you would eventually find such a friend boring. What's missing? *Fidelity.* Your professional friend has no true loyalty, because the friendship is likely to end when the money stops. And there is no fidelity to truth, since the friendship is based on deception. Maybe your self-esteem would go up for a time in such a phony friendship, but it would plummet fast if you found out about the deception. Your self would not grow richer and deeper, and the self you might be incorporating would be the self of a flatterer and a charlatan.

Of course, your parents would never come up with such a dumb idea. They know the self you want to form is a self oriented toward truth, and fidelity to the truth. And, as you indicated by show of hands a few minutes ago, you want honest friends who will tell you the truth.

Teaching, friendship, and honor codes

Do you think you could have such a friendship (a friendship oriented toward truth) with your college teachers, at least some of them? [Most members of the audience raised their hand]. I'm glad your answer is yes, both for your benefit, and theirs.

The University of Virginia has a newspaper called the *Cavalier Daily*. Two years ago I read a letter to the editor by a graduating senior, Katie Dalton. She wrote about her best teacher, William Fishback:

> My friendship with you has been the most rewarding relationship to come out of my academic experience. You know just how and when to push me out of procrastination, and you consistently offer support as a father would. More than anyone else, you embody the Jeffersonian ideal of a professor who instructs but also encourages his students, and who values friendships with his pupils as much as their final exams.

Virginia is an honor code school--one of the original honor code schools. I think honor codes foster friendships between students and teachers. In a moment I'll try to explain why.

First, I want to stress that not only can you be friends with your teachers, but forming genuine friendships with them (at least some of them) is something you should do, as an important part of your education. Seek them out. Show up at office hours and ask good questions. Tell them something about yourself, including any of your doubts or fears about college life or career choices.

The idea that teachers and students can be friends in the pursuit of truth goes back to the time of Plato's academy. Socrates was the teacher of Plato and Plato was the teacher of Aristotle. Friendship was at the core of their relationships, even when Plato and Aristotle disagreed about philosophical issues. Between them there was no conflict between fidelity to truth and fidelity to each other, because the mutual pursuit of truth was the core of the friendship.

What does all this have to do with your new honor code?
Properly designed and administered, an honor code reflects a partnership between faculty members and students. The partnership is explicitly designed to foster an orientation toward truth. In this sense it's a larger manifestation of the kind of friendship seen between UVA student Katie Dalton and her teacher William Fishback.

The immediate beneficiary of the faculty-student honor code partnership is the university itself. The student voice is heard in ways that might have been overlooked before. New ideas are generated, and new insights gained. A climate of trust and cooperation is more likely to evolve.

The larger society also benefits, because honor code schools seem particularly effective in emphasizing the importance of social trust. Remember the example of the ceiling above our heads.

But probably the biggest beneficiary of a faculty-student partnership in pursuit of truth (if you take your new honor code seriously) is *you*. You'll be building a self oriented toward truth-seeking and truth-telling. Doing so will enrich your lives in many ways. Perhaps the most important is that you will discover the highest kind of friendship--friendship grounded in *fidelity*, in the full sense of that word.

Belief + Doubt = Sanity

By *Gary Pavela*

*Adapted from Gary Pavela's Law and Policy Report
(March 25, 2016) and MEDIUM (February 1, 2022)*

The American Bar Association definition of a "judicial temperament" refers to "compassion, decisiveness, open-mindedness, sensitivity, courtesy, patience, freedom from bias and commitment to equal justice."

Are those qualities compatible? For example, how does one combine "open-mindedness" with "decisiveness?"

This question is posed and answered in a work by conceptual artist Barbara Kruger, on display at Hirshhorn Museum and Sculpture Garden in Washington, D.C.

"BELIEF + DOUBT = SANITY" Creative Commons link

"Sanity" encompasses cognition and emotion (especially empathy); it reflects humility about possessing ultimate knowledge. The capacity to trust and gain insight from others may be the best evidence of sanity we can display.

The methodology of science--one of humanity's most transformative conceptual inventions--is grounded on this view. Scientists display *humility* by starting with a question rather than a dogmatic assertion. The question prompts thought and inquiry leading to a *belief.* The belief is then stated as a *hypothesis.* The hypothesis is challenged by *disciplined doubt* (empirical examination and openness to criticism). The result is actionable *truth*, always open to evidence-based correction and reformulation.

The methodology of science is a comparatively recent human creation. It remains vulnerable, as evidenced by the authoritarian hubris, rhetorical passion, and personal invective on display in contemporary politics. Each "side" (left and right) blames the other for those unfortunate traits--and neither side (sharing a common human nature) is immune to them.

How do we teach and preserve the "sanity" of humility, disciplined doubt, and a willingness to act on beliefs while remaining subject to correction?

One answer includes *appreciation for tested methodologies* (e.g. understanding "due process" as a disciplined truth-seeking mechanism, not a "legalistic" inconvenience) and *habituation* in practicing them ("hear the case before you decide it").

We also suggested in a previous issue that the methodology of science might provide a sense of purpose (*TPR* 13.48). That view was stated by the American philosopher John Dewey in a February 6, 1924 essay in *The New Republic* ("Fundamentals," p. 275):

> Those . . . who have arrogated to themselves the title of fundamentalists recognize of course no mean between their dogmas and . . . hopeless uncertainty . . . .

> [They are not] aware that there are a steadily increasing number
> of persons who find security in methods of inquiry, of observa-
> tion, experiment, of forming and following working hypotheses.
> Such persons are not unsettled by the upsetting of any special
> belief, because they retain security of procedure. They can say,
> borrowing language from another context, "though this method
> slay my most cherished belief, yet will I trust it."

Nobel-Prize winning physicist Richard Feynman said something similar in this marvelous, short BBC video (1981; please click the video
link and take a moment to hear his actual words; transcription by
Antti Yrjönen):

> You see, one thing is I can live with doubt and uncertainty and
> not knowing. I think it is much more *interesting* to live not
> knowing than to have answers which might be wrong. *I have
> approximate answers and possible beliefs and different degrees of
> certainty about different things; but I am not absolutely sure of
> anything* and of many things I do not know anything about;
> such as whether it means anything to ask why we are here and
> what the question might mean. I might think about it a little,
> but if I cannot figure it out then I go to something else. But I
> do not have to know an answer; I do not feel frightened by not
> knowing things, by being lost in the mysterious universe with-
> out having any purpose, which is the way it really is as far as
> I can tell, possibly. It does not frighten me [emphasis added].

Affirming these principles to our students is best accomplished by example (how we treat them and our colleagues). But it also helps to
identify admirable lives that exhibit comparable qualities. Historical
examples include Plato (who emphasized the importance of dialogue
rather than rhetoric); Nelson Mandela (who proclaimed in one of his
most famous speeches that "I have been influenced in my thinking by
both West and East. All this has led me to feel that in my search for a
political formula, I should be absolutely impartial and objective"); the
authors of the United States Constitution (who created a document
that challenged any claim to perfection by incorporating a procedure

for amendment); and Judge Learned Hand's famous observation that "The spirit of liberty is the spirit which is not too sure that it is right."

Overall, perhaps the best example of humility, disciplined doubt, and a willingness to act without the pretense of absolute truth is Abraham Lincoln. Please consider these words in his Second Inaugural Address

> Neither party expected for the war the magnitude or the duration which it has already attained. Neither anticipated that the cause of the conflict might cease with or even before the conflict itself should cease. Each looked for an easier triumph, and a result less fundamental and astounding. Both read the same Bible and pray to the same God, and each invokes His aid against the other. It may seem strange that any men should dare to ask a just God's assistance in wringing their bread from the sweat of other men's faces, but let us judge not, that we be not judged. The prayers of both could not be answered. That of neither has been answered fully. *The Almighty has His own purposes . . . .*
>
> *With malice toward none, with charity for all, with firmness in the right as God gives us to see the right,* let us strive on to finish the work we are in, to bind up the nation's wounds, to care for him who shall have borne the battle and for his widow and his orphan, to do all which may achieve and cherish a just and lasting peace among ourselves and with all nations [emphases added].

In his book "The Irony of American History" theologian Reinhold Niebuhr suggested that Lincoln's "brooding sense of charity" came not from any dogmatic claim to truth, but from life experiences that produced a humble and "contrite heart." In this context, we might include the capacity for charity as another component of the "sanity" Barbara Kruger had in mind.